ICELAND

Travel with Marco Polo Insider Tips

INSIDER TIP
Your shortcut to a great experience

MARCO POLO TOP HIGHLIGHTS

HARPA ★1

The multicoloured glass façade of the concert hall plays enchantingly with both natural and artificial light.

Tip: The staircase windows make for a great shot.

➤ p. 44, Reykjavík

ÞINGVELLIR ★2

The birthplace of Iceland – where both free state and republic were proclaimed (photo).

➤ p. 52, Reykjavík

GEYSIR ★3

The Geysir and its little brother Strokkur regularly shoot out jets of water.

Tip: Catch the swell just before it erupts.

➤ p. 61, The South

HEKLA ★4

Iceland's most active volcano spits fire from time to time, which is why it was known for centuries as the gateway to hell.

➤ p. 63, The South

JÖKULSÁRLÓN ★5

Channel your inner James Bond and take a boat trip between shimmering icebergs to experience the magic of this icy paradise.

➤ p. 72, The East

MÝVATN 6

This lake is home to lava sculptures, volcanic craters … and all the country's duck species.

Tip: The midnight sun envelops the lake and its islands in magic.

➤ p. 82, The North

DETTIFOSS 7

With water thundering 44m into the Jökulsárgljúfur Gorge below, Europe's largest waterfall could be a younger brother to the Niagara Falls.

➤ p. 83, The North

DYNJANDI 8

In the northwest, the multiple cascades of Iceland's most beautiful waterfall flow down in the shape of a fan.

Tip: Shoot with a long exposure to capture the haze.

➤ p. 94, The West

LÁTRABJARG 9

The country's westernmost cliff stretches for 14km and is home to thousands of seabirds. The sea rages some 400m below.

Tip: Get down to eye level with the birds.

➤ p. 95, The West

ASKJA 10

The caldera is a natural monument crowned at its centre with Iceland's second-deepest lake.

➤ p. 113, The Highlands

CONTENTS

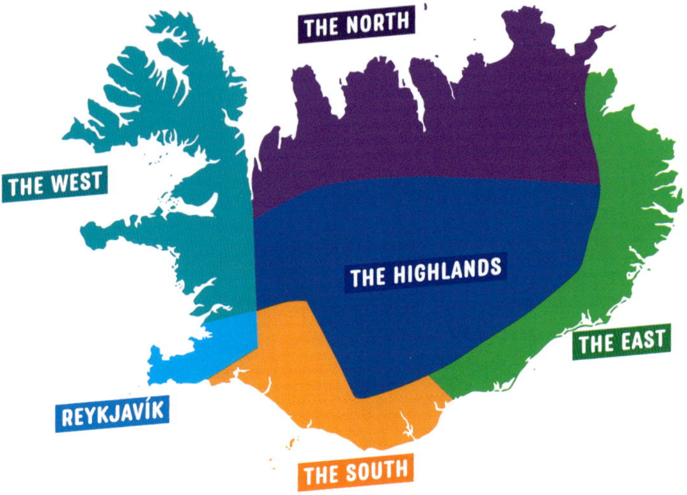
THE NORTH
THE WEST
THE HIGHLANDS
THE EAST
REYKJAVÍK
THE SOUTH

CONTENTS

Plan your visit
£–£££ Price categories
Eating/drinking
Shopping
Going out
Rainy day activities
Budget activities
Family activities
Classic experiences

(A2) Refers to the removable pull-out map
(a2) Refers to the inset street maps on the pull-out map

BEST OF ICELAND

Iceland's traditional turf roofs blend perfectly into the landscape

BEST WHEN IT RAINS

ACTIVITIES TO BRIGHTEN YOUR DAY

MUSIC IN CHURCH

During the summer months there are regular lunchtime concerts in the *Hallgrímskirkja* in Reykjavík. The church's acoustics are outstanding, and the bright interior is pleasantly unfussy (photo).

➤ p. 45, Reykjavík

UNDER ONE ROOF

A rainy day is an ideal opportunity to do some shopping and perhaps see a new film in its original language. Shopping malls *Kringlan* in Reykjavík and *Smáralind* in Kópavogur have heaps of shops and giant cinemas.

➤ p. 48, Reykjavík

WATER EVERYWHERE

Reykjavík is not only home to the large, well-known *Laugardalur* thermal baths, but plenty of others, too. And sitting in a cosy hot pot (a small pool with geothermally heated water) in rain or snow is a real treat. Should the breeze around your ears turn chilly, just put your head under the warm water.

➤ p. 49, Reykjavík

A STROLL ON THE BEACH

What is probably Iceland's most stunning beach, *Dyrhólaós*, lies to the west of Vík. The water gurgles as it washes over the black lava pebbles, and you can walk for miles. Waterproofs will protect you from the sea spray.

➤ p. 67, The South

THE MAGIC OF THE GLACIERS

An installation of glacier-water specimens in glass columns, combined with a fine view, can be found at the "Library of Water", *Vatnasafn* in Stykkishólmur. This place invites quiet contemplation – it's all the work of artist Roni Horn.

➤ p. 96, The West

BEST ON A BUDGET

FOR SMALLER WALLETS

EXPLORING REYKJAVÍK

The *Reykjavík City Card* is the best and cheapest way to explore the entire capital. It's good for swimming, too: simply show your card to gain free entry to all the city's swimming pools.

➤ p. 44, Reykjavík

WHAT'S GEOTHERMICS ALL ABOUT?

At several sites in the town of *Hveragerði*, you can see how geothermal energy is being harnessed to heat greenhouses and outdoor beds in the horticultural school. Head to the *thermal area* for information about the different kinds of steam and thermal springs (photo).

➤ p. 58, The South

DOWN ON THE FARM

It may seem gloomy inside the 11th-century *Stöng* longhouse, but you will quickly get used to it as you explore the ruins of the old farmhouse. It's one of Iceland's few remaining buildings from the Middle Ages and was buried by pumice ash for centuries following a volcanic eruption. It's worth a detour from Route 32 to see it on your way to the Highlands.

➤ p. 111, The Highlands

RETURN TRANSFER TO THE AIRPORT

If you buy an online *Flybus ticket* from and to the airport, you'll pay considerably less than purchasing two single tickets. It's well worth planning ahead and it's easy too!

➤ p. 124, Good to know

SALAD DAYS

Do as the Reykjavík natives do and enjoy a salad bowl for lunch in one of the city's many *salad bars* – generous, healthy and very reasonable (2,000–2,800 ISK). You'll also find salad bars in grocery stores like Nóatún, Hagkaup or Nýkaup.

BEST WITH CHILDREN

FUN FOR YOUNG & OLD

UP CLOSE WITH THE ANIMALS

See Iceland's animals – including seals, greylag geese, reindeer, mink and arctic foxes – up close at the *Reykjavík Family Park and Zoo. Daily summer 10am–6pm, winter 10am–5pm | admission 980 ISK, children (5–12 years) 750 ISK | Engjavegur | mu.is*

HOT & COLD

How does a volcano work? What is lava? Why is ice blue? Find the answers to these questions and more at the "Wonders of Iceland" exhibition in the *Perlan* natural history museum. Here you can learn about everything from glacier caves and the Northern Lights to the sea and volcanoes.

➤ p. 47, Reykjavík

RIDING

Most Icelandic horses are friendly creatures and, what's more, you're not too far from the ground when you sit on them! Located mainly in southern Iceland, riding stables such as *Elðhestar* in Vellir are perfect for young and old alike, including beginners.

➤ p. 58, The South

ICEBERGS YOU CAN TOUCH

On the *Jökulsárlón* glacier lagoon, you can sail around the huge icebergs and even suck on a piece of ice.

➤ p. 72, The East

SPOT SEALS & WHALES

The west coast of the Vatnsnes peninsula is a great place to see seals lying on the rocks and on the beach – their favourite spots are near Svalbarð and Illugastaðir (photo). In *Húsavík*, you can take a *whale-watching boat trip*.

➤ p. 84, The North

CAVING

Explore the depths of Iceland's *lava caves* with a lamp and helmet. Did you know people used to live in them?

➤ p. 107, The Highlands

BEST

CLASSIC EXPERIENCES

ONLY IN ICELAND

GREAT KNITS

The traditional Iceland pullover is an ideal piece of outdoor kit, and at *Víkurprjón* in Vík they have a huge selection of handknitted models with the typical pattern around the neck. Alternatively, in true Icelandic spirit, you can always knit your own.

➤ p. 31, Shopping

DANCE ON A VOLCANO

The island of *Heimaey* is a prime example of how the consequences of nature's menacing power can be turned to man's advantage: the hot lava heats the water; the ruins and excavations from a 1973 eruption are tourist attractions. The island's residents are also happy that their port is protected by a fortress of lava.

➤ p. 63, The South

SEETHING EARTH

In some places in Iceland the earth's crust is relatively thin, hence the bubbling, hissing and steaming. If there's also an element of sulphur involved, then you're in for an extra aromatic experience, as at *Námaskarð* near Mývatn.

➤ p. 82, The North

CASCADING WATERS

Iceland is synonymous with waterfalls; there are thousands of them, many marvelled at daily, others completely hidden from view. The finest is probably the fan-shaped *Dynjandi* (The Thundering One), in the northwest (photo).

➤ p. 94, The West

LAVA DESERTS

Iceland is a land of volcanoes which erupt regularly, resulting in ash clouds and lava flows. The country's beautiful lava-and-boulder deserts, for example *Ódáðahraun* in the Highlands, have evolved over centuries.

➤ p. 111, The Highlands

GET TO KNOW ICELAND

Rainbow colours on the street in peaceful Seyðisfjörður

DISCOVER ICELAND

If you plan to visit the mighty Dettifoss waterfall, be sure to wear waterproofs!

Iceland is full of contradictions, surprises and secrets. Its ancient volcanic landscape transports you back to the time of the earth's origins. Large glaciers lie dormant, stunning lava beaches hug the coastline, countless waterfalls thunder into the depths below, and toasty hot springs practically beg you to take a dip.

NATURE, NATURE AND MORE NATURE

First and foremost, it is the varied face of the landscape that draws tourists to this island in the North Atlantic. In the country's south, you'll find expansive meadows and broad, black beaches washed by crashing white surf; close by, the black snouts of giant glaciers seem to run out of steam just before reaching the sea. In the east, steep basalt plateaux surge upwards; deep fjords and narrow mountain

874 Ingólfur Arnarson settles permanently in Iceland

930 Founding of the Althing (parliament) and declaration of a free and independent Icelandic state

1000 Adoption of Christianity

1380 Iceland comes under Danish rule

1874 A new constitution reinstates the Althing

1918 Union treaty between Denmark and Iceland

gorges have cut a path through them. Wide valleys and the country's longest fjord, the Eyjafjörður, dominate the north. The northwest, scored by numerous fjords to form its characteristic jagged coastline, is only sparsely populated. Landslides, which at the very least block a few roads, are common during the harsh winters. The higher ground is a broad lava field scattered with boulders, an inhospitable moonscape of isolated peaks and mountain ranges. Add to this the hundreds of waterfalls: hidden, thundering, mighty and beautiful – some of them well known, others so small you might be the first to stumble across them. All this dramatic scenery is concentrated on a single island whose closest neighbours are Greenland, 300km to the northwest, and the Faroe Islands, 500km to the southeast.

Iceland is also a land of peace – there are endless places to experience the intensity of hearing nothing but the sounds of nature, whether that is the whoosh of the waves as they run over the pebbles on the beach, the rushing of a waterfall or a chorus of birdsong.

AN ANGRY ISLAND

In some places, the earth's crust is dangerously thin, and the bubbling, steaming holes give you a glimpse of our planet's fiery interior. What people in the Middle Ages held to be simply threatening and strange – the work of the Devil and the gateway to Hell – is used by 21st-century Icelanders to great advantage. The lava serves as building material; geothermal energy is transformed into electricity,

- **1944** Declaration of the Republic of Iceland in Þingvellir
- **1952–74** Cod Wars: confrontations with the UK over fishing rights
- **1994 / 2001** Entry into the European Economic Area (EEA) and the Schengen Agreement
- **2008** Financial and banking crisis brings the country to the brink of bankruptcy
- **2016** The prime minister resigns over the Panama Papers scandal
- **2022** Post-pandemic tourism boom; volcanic eruption on the Reykjanes peninsula

and the hot water heats houses and swimming pools. The Icelanders have learnt how to "dance on a volcano". The country's true wealth lies in its natural resources, which are fundamental to the existence of the 370,000 people who live here.

A LOOK BACK IN TIME

The Icelanders love their island and its breathtaking landscape, which has formed them just as much as their history. To this day, they still consider themselves the true descendants of the Vikings. First attempts at settlement failed; the daring Norseman Flóki thought the terrain too forbidding and icy, prompting him to give it the name Ísland (Iceland). He came ashore in the northwest in CE 865 and stayed just one winter. Only ten years later, however, the island was permanently settled. The next 300 years, today referred to by Icelanders as the "Golden Age", saw a blossoming of culture. But dark times set in after 1380. Under the Danish crown, free trade was limited; national self-determination was a thing of the past; and a host of natural disasters devastated the country. Famines, epidemics and extreme poverty were the result. Independence was achieved – finally – in 1944.

NATURE CREATES WEALTH

Iceland is a modern country, and some visitors may be a little disappointed to find that its people no longer live in little turf-covered houses, but often in high-rise blocks built to withstand earthquakes. However, the leap into the modern era only really happened with the US occupation during World War II, when Reykjavík grew exponentially. Even today, construction is a common sight in the capital. Iceland's economy, meanwhile, is based on energy, its fishing grounds and steadily growing tourism. Iceland welcomes visitors all year round. In summer, when three months of daylight are the attraction, hardly anyone seems to sleep, and many work outside until midnight. During this period, the flora truly bursts into life. The midnight sun, low in the sky, transforms the landscape into an enchanted golden realm and paints the glacier-topped mountains in glowing deep red and violet hues. In September and early October, autumnal colours dominate, and the hillsides and plains resemble multicoloured patchwork blankets. During the long winter nights, you can often marvel at the fascinating spectacle of the dancing Northern Lights – magical, mystical and bewitching.

ALWAYS SOMETHING GOING ON

If you're on the hunt for adventure, you'll find it in Iceland. Whether it's a trip up to the glaciers and into the ice and lava caves, jeep rides in the Highlands, rafting on icy rivers, riding an Icelandic horse, or watching for puffins. Maybe its days of hiking in the island's solitude. With so much choice, you're sure to find the right thing for you. And even without the latest volcanic eruption, there's one thing Iceland certainly isn't: boring.

AT A GLANCE

368,800
Population

Stoke-on-Trent: 392,000

99.2 %

Households with internet access

United Kingdom: 95%

6,088km
Coastline

UK's total coastline: 17,820km

103,000km²
area

England 130,279km²

LARGEST GLACIER: VATNAJÖKULL

8,300km² surface area

WARMEST MONTHS

JULY/ AUGUST 13°C

MOST POPULAR TIME TO TRAVEL

JUNE– AUGUST

AREA OF VATNAJÖKULL NATIONAL PARK: 14.347KM²

REYKJAVÍK

Biggest city, with approx. 130,000 inhabitants

MOST FAMOUS PEOPLE
Leifur Eiríksson
Björk

850 CARS PER 1,000 INHABITANTS

UNDERSTAND ICELAND

AMERICA

Why is Iceland's international airport named after Leifur Eiríksson? Because he "discovered" America long before Columbus, after his legendary father, Erik the Red, had discovered and conquered Greenland in CE 982. From there, Leifur sailed west in CE 1000, hoping to find new land. He put ashore at three different locations in what is now Canada, naming them Helluland, Markland and Vínland. Some years later, other Icelanders tried to settle in Vínland, but because of conflicts with the Native Americans they returned to Iceland three years later. However, the shipping route to the New World continued to be used for collecting timber. These journeys were documented in the Icelandic sagas, which were later presumably read by Columbus.

HOT POTS

Hot pots – small pools with geothermically heated water piped in, often beside a lake or outside a summer house – are one of the country's major attractions, alongside its natural thermal lakes that are popular for swimming. Most houses have their own hot pot, and the same was true back in medieval times. Politician and poet Snorri Sturluson (1179–1241) was an early fan of consultations in his hot pot, Snorralaug, in the village of Reykholt, which he had specially built for this purpose. Discussions and meetings are more fruitful in a relaxed atmosphere which is why, even today, these baths bring together politicians and managers, poets and singers; they are the place to exchange news and views. Just like most outdoor activities in Iceland, you can enjoy communal outdoor bathing all year round, irrespective of wind and weather. Is there anything better than sitting in a hot pot enjoying a drink while it is snowing around you?

Just for the record: Snorri was murdered on his way between Snorralaug and his house in 1241. Conclusion: it's safer to stay put in the hot pot!

GREEN POWER

Iceland is considered a global leader in terms of renewable energy. All of its electricity is generated from hydro- and geothermal power. This is no surprise, really, when you consider the abundant supply of both on the island. Geothermal energy is used in the form of superheated steam or hot water. Almost 90 per cent of households are heated in this way, as are over 200,000m² of greenhouse space, fish breeding stations, swimming pools and streets (yes, some of Reykjavík's busiest streets and pavements are heated).

However, the picture is very different when the country's overall electricity consumption is examined: Icelanders have the highest per capita electricity consumption in the world, with over 53,000kWh per person. Private households are not solely to blame for this. The country's industry is the major sinner, in particular the

Icelandic horses have thick winter coats to protect them from the harsh climate

aluminium-smelting plants, which compromise the island's environmental role-model status. Thousands of nautical miles are covered to import the world's main source of aluminium, bauxite, which is smelted here. Vast areas of the Highlands have disappeared under water, for example with the Kárahnjúkar Dam in the northeast, to produce energy for smelting.

From an environmental perspective, it makes far more sense to use the country's energy to produce food. Since the financial crisis in 2008, there has been a drive to produce more regionally grown vegetables in greenhouses. In addition, you can see cautious attempts at cultivating arable crops and, of course, potatoes.

ANIMAL INHABITANTS

The island is home to the cute, furry Icelandic horse. Although you'll be tempted to stroke them, it's worth knowing that their owners do not usually appreciate you doing so. There are actually more "Isis" – as the Icelandic horse is popularly known – living abroad than in their native Iceland. In former days, horses were the only means of transport on the island, and today they are used for tourism purposes and for rounding up sheep.

The herds of wandering sheep are a mainstay of the island's economy. In summer you can spot them roaming across the countryside, even in the most faraway corners. There are around 400,000 sheep in Iceland, and both their meat and wool are used.

Where there are sheep, there are dogs, and they will always give visitors an enthusiastic welcome when they drive up to a farmhouse because they generally love visitors. The Icelandic sheepdog is similar to the Welsh corgi, a friendly, long-haired breed full of energy: a classic herding dog.

The Arctic fox is the only land mammal that was native to Iceland before human settlement, and is now commonly found in the northwest.

However, Iceland is a paradise for birds. Tens of thousands of seabirds nest on the steep rocky cliffs: black guillemot, razorbill, fulmar, gannet, guillemot and puffin. Inland, there are huge colonies of pink-footed geese, while rare species of European duck, such as the harlequin and long-tailed varieties, splash about on Lake Mývatn. You can also often see the large bluish-black ravens – they are said to keep the god Odin informed about what the people are doing.

EVERYTHING IN THE SEA ...

... is good enough to eat. Or that's what the Icelanders believed for hundreds of years. Today, their diet is still largely made up of fish and shellfish, and the export of seafood plays an important role in the island's economy. Annual quotas are laid down to preserve stocks of the most important species fished – cod, haddock, redfish, saithe and capelin. High-tech processing plants operate with flexible production systems so they can react quickly to market demands. The main export regions are the USA, Japan and Europe.

For centuries, sea mammals were hunted for their meat, and although the hunting of minke whales is still permitted, most Icelanders are now conscious of the senselessness of this

Catch of the day at Arnarstapi harbour

activity. Much better to spot minke whales and orcas (killer whales) on whale-watching excursions, when you can see porpoises, too. On the coast, you will often come across various species of seal, which also breed here.

COLOURFUL FLORA

Even in the most remote Highland settings, you'll find a diverse variety of plants and flowers. Most species are tiny, but with intensely bright flowers. Colourful meadows full of a variety of herbaceous plants, such as the purple cranesbill, thrive on the mountain slopes. On the barren plains you'll find varieties of saxifrage, for example the pink moss campion, and along river banks the glowing purple blossoms of the Arctic fireweed and carpets of green moss. Berries, fungi and brown-grey-green lichen *fjallagras* also enrich the Icelandic menu. Icelandic moss shimmers grey-green and is very soft; it is also highly valued for its healing properties.

INSIDER TIP
Healing power of moss

In early summer, Iceland transforms into the "blue island" when the widespread Nootka lupine (Alsakan lupin) blossoms. Introduced to combat erosion and help with reforestation, these plants have colonised vegetated areas and overtaken the natural flora. Nevertheless, the country's reforestation programme has been a major success and the island is no longer a barren outcrop.

CREATIVITY HOTSPOT

Iceland doesn't only rate as a land of literature with a passion for reading, it

TRUE OR FALSE?

AN ISLAND OF ELVES?

Everybody knows about them and yet they're hardly ever seen. Iceland's elves live hidden away in rocks and boulders, allowing only a select few seers to catch a glimpse of them. The elves' desire to preserve their rocky world means they've been known to destroy construction machinery and even cause injuries when new roads or buildings threaten their habitat. Legend has it that the town of Hafnarfjörður is home to the country's biggest elf population. If you ask Icelanders whether they believe in the *huldufólk,* or "hidden people" (as the elves are known), few will admit to it, but actually many don't doubt their existence.

THE EASY LIFE

Icelanders don't have a typically north European attitude to time-keeping. A certain nonchalance is the norm here, not punctuality! *"Þetta reddast",* or "We'll manage" is the order of the day. You'll soon find this laid-back attitude is a good thing, especially as the saying holds good for bumps in the road, too. Icelanders are fantastic at improvising and being truly flexible. And while it might seem incredible at first, things really do always seem to work out in the end.

has become an exciting place for music, creative arts and design. Everybody knows who Björk and Sigur Rós are, and every year music agents travel to the Iceland Airwaves Festival to hear the latest Icelandic sounds.

INSIDER TIP
Music made in Iceland

Have you ever listened to the album *Steingervingur* by Steinunn Jónsdóttir? Her band is called asdfhg., and her high-pitched voice and electronic sound might remind you of Sigur Rós – give it a listen!

Icelandic artists tend not to restrict themselves to one genre. For example, Hallgrímur Helgason is both an author and a painter. Artists are often politically active, too, a fact underlined when the author and comedian Jón Gnarr became mayor of Reykjavík (2010–14).

Iceland's designers like to use local materials for their creations. The Icelandic Design Centre aims to both raise awareness and appreciation of Icelandic design within the country and promote exports and collaborations with industry.

SONS AND DAUGHTERS

Names in Iceland are a conundrum for foreigners. Most are difficult to pronounce, but luckily you only need to learn the first name as people address each other by their first name only in Iceland. The second name is the father's name with the suffix *-son* (son) or *-dóttir* (daughter). The names in a typical family could look something like this: father Einar Jóhannson and mother Svava Elíasdóttir have a son, Gísli Einarsson, and a daughter, Jórunn Einarsdóttir. As you can see, there is no common family name, only patronyms (names derived from the father's name).

FROM CO_2 TO STONE

Icelanders are an innovative lot. Back in September 2021, the country commissioned the world's largest plant for storing carbon dioxide from the air. Around 4,000 tonnes of carbon dioxide, equivalent to emissions from 870 cars, can be stored annually. While this process is pretty energy- and water-intensive, luckily Iceland has plenty of both – the plant is handily located next to the Nesjavellir geothermal power plant. The filtered gas is dissolved in water and then pumped to a depth of 1,000m, where it comes into contact with minerals, causing the carbon dioxide to fossilise and remain there.

VOLCANIC ACTIVITY

At 15–20 million years old, Iceland is one of the youngest areas of the world from a geological point of view – and it is still evolving. Volcanic activity, seething thermal zones, earthquakes and the constant drifting apart of two major continental plates are changing Iceland's landscape all the time. The active volcanic belt traverses the country from Reykjanes in the southwest to Öxarfjörður in the northeast. There are two more such areas on the Snæfellsnes peninsula and in the south.

For geologists, Iceland is like an illustrated textbook, featuring many types of volcano and rock formations,

Energy produced at the Nesjavellir geothermal plant powers the nearby CO_2 storage facility

such as ropy lava and obsidian, as well as thermal areas, solfataras (sulphur vents) and geysers. Most of the 30 or more volcanic systems in these areas have a central volcano or a mountain range with a caldera (a large, round crater caused by volcanic eruption, such as at Askja).

Since the settlement of the island, around 250 eruptions, some of them lasting months or years, have taken place in 15 volcanic systems. Some 45,000m³ of lava rock has been created in the process. The most active central volcanoes are Hekla, Katla and Grímsvötn, each one clocking up over 20 eruptions. In 2010, the eruption of the volcano Eyjafjallajökull brought European air traffic to a standstill for several weeks. Between August 2014 and February 2015, Bárðarbunga spewed up to 30m³ of lava into the air, while the 2023–24 Sundhnúkur eruptions brought lava flows close to the town of Grindavik.

STATISTICS

Icelanders love statistics, which is not something that can be said of many nations. The island regularly publishes its figures for the latest fish catches, but other numbers are much more interesting. For example, how many Icelandic opera singers sing at La Scala in Milan? Only one, but when you consider the size of the population it's quite an achievement! But such comparisons make the statistic that, in 2016, 600 Icelanders were named in the Panama Papers, the leaked documents revealing the identities of tax evaders, even more shocking. Revelations that leading politicians had illegal offshore tax arrangements led to widespread protests and, eventually, a new government.

EATING SHOPPING SPORT

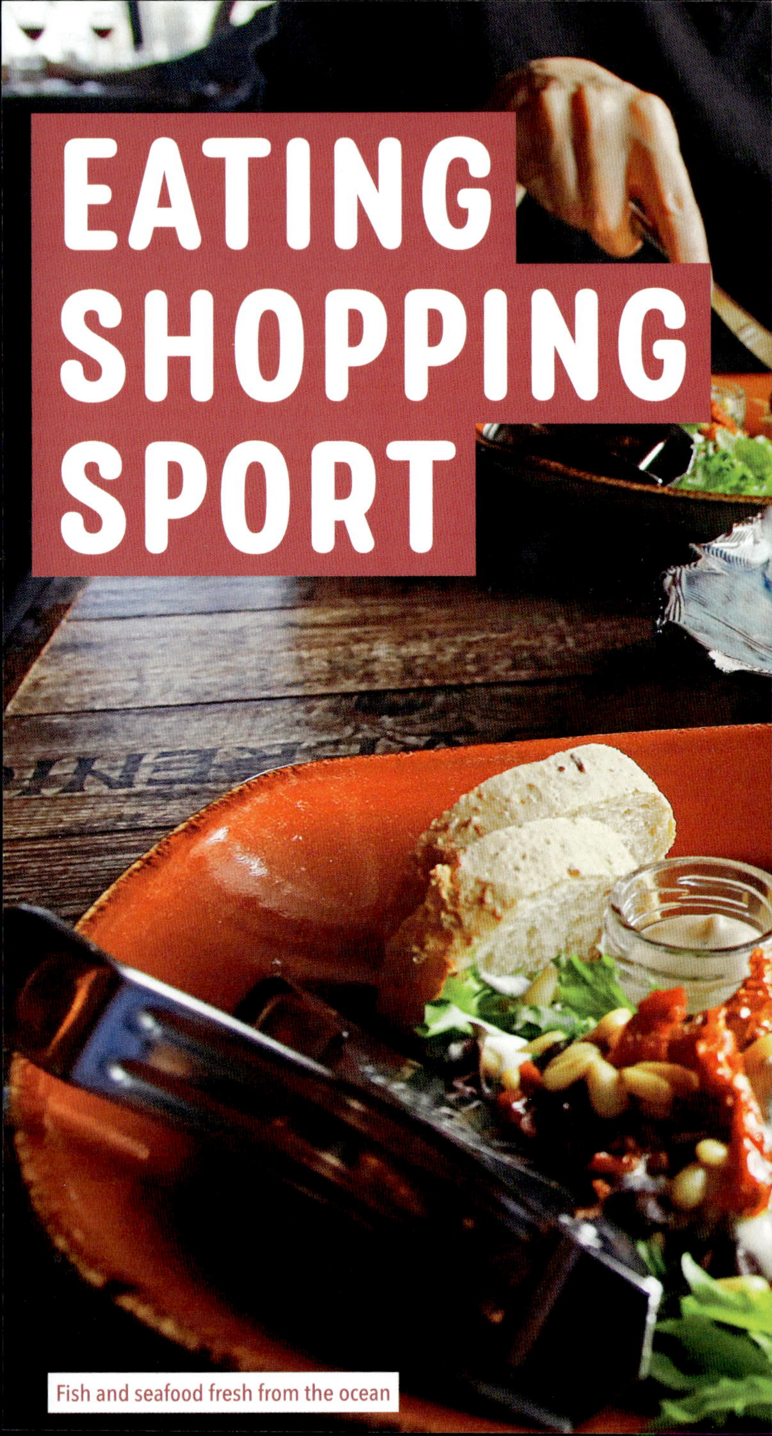

Fish and seafood fresh from the ocean

EATING & DRINKING

Fish, fish and ... more fish! Whether it's dried cod or wild salmon, Iceland's chefs have got the fruits of the sea down to a fine art. They love to borrow from traditional cuisine and to breathe new life into dishes with vegetables, herbs and spices – things that weren't available in the good old days!

Traditionally, Icelandic cooking is simple and down-to-earth: fish, meat, potatoes, cereals and milk products. Various techniques have been used to preserve fish and meat, including souring, smoking, drying, curing or pickling in whey. Some old recipes have lived on into the present day and are eaten at the winter's end feast known as *þorrablót*. For the Icelanders it's a way of driving out the winter. Eating foods preserved in the traditional manner harks back to earlier centuries and marks the return of fresh foods to the table.

Young cooks are reviving old recipes or adapting them, for example, horsemeat is sometimes used instead of lamb for smoked *hangikjöt*. To experience the best of Icelandic cuisine, it's definitely worth seeking out traditional restaurants and regional dishes.

A GREENHOUSE FOR GREENS

Local production of tomatoes, cucumbers, peppers, lettuce and mushrooms only began with the construction of greenhouses. Until then, only rhubarb and cabbage had been grown. Now, some supermarkets have an impressive range of fresh vegetables and fruit, imported from all over the world. The addition of traditionally frowned upon "greens" has enriched the Icelandic diet, which previously consisted largely of meat and fish. This newly varied diet is also reflected in the range of places to eat – from Asian restaurants to fast-food chains and

Enjoy a beer at the bar, followed by a tasty local fish dish

rustic Viking pubs, you'll find just about everything here.

When the 2008 economic crisis hit, the trend towards regional cooking was embraced in Iceland. The import of food was extremely expensive at the time as a result of the collapse of currency, so the cultivation of vegetables in greenhouses expanded. Even cereals are now being cultivated, made possible by climate change and the creation of cold-resistant grains.

FOR THE CARNIVORES

Where both fish and meat are concerned, quality is a top priority, and all products are from home-reared animals. Almost everything from the rivers and the sea lands on a plate in some form or other. Apart from the usual sources of meat, foal is also on the menu, and, in the poultry department, *svartfugl* (razorbill), whose large, colourful eggs also appear on the shelves in spring. Some supermarkets have fresh meat and fish counters, otherwise prepacked products are to be found on refrigerated shelves. There are a number of small, independent fishmongers in Reykjavík, which also sell auk and their eggs in season. In some places, you can buy freshly caught fish from the fishermen as they come in to harbour.

INSIDER TIP
Razorbill eggs

WHAT'S ON THE MENU?

Icelanders love eating – and in great quantities; meals are lavish. A decent breakfast buffet includes cornflakes with *súrmjólk* (soured milk) and brown sugar, bread, a selection of cold meats, jam – made, perhaps, from home-grown berries – tomatoes, cucumber and of course *síld* (herring), marinated in a variety of sauces.

At lunchtime most of the working population go out to eat. Restaurants

Indulge in a sweet treat at a Reykjavík café

put on appropriate menus, consisting of soup and a fish dish for a reasonable price of around 2,960 króna (£17). Among the more popular choices are *ýsa* (haddock), *þorskur* (cod) and *karfi* (redfish), either steamed or grilled.

AFTERNOON SNACKTIME

In the afternoon, you'll find a range of cakes, catering to both sweet and savoury tastes. The impressive-looking creamy gateaux are loaded with calories, whereas the *pönnukökur* (crêpes), filled with cream or jam, and *kleinur* (doughnuts) are only a little lighter. *Flatbrauð* is a pancake made out of rye flour, served topped with a thin slice of *hangikjöt* (smoked lamb). Sandwiches with *rækja* (shrimps) and mayonnaise are also popular afternoon snacks.

EVENING INDULGENCE

Evening meals are mostly eaten with family and are the most important of the day. At the weekend, many Icelanders like to round off the week with a visit to a restaurant. A number of internationally trained chefs create highly imaginative dishes from local produce, often inspired by Asian or Mediterranean cuisine.

The salmon is excellent, whether smoked or grilled. Farmed salmon is available all year round, and in summer the wild variety is fished from the salmon rivers for which Iceland is famous. *Reyktur silunguris* (smoked trout) is a speciality of the region around Mývatn, and tastes particularly tangy as it is smoked over juniper wood.

Should you choose *lamb* as your main course, you'll have to pay considerably more than for fish (around 5,925 króna or £34), but it's worth it. The lambs roam freely across the meadows in summer, eating only grasses and herbs, which is why their meat has a slightly "seasoned" flavour.

Another speciality is *hreindýr* (reindeer) – for venison aficionados it's a real treat. You'll still come across restaurants advertising *hvalur* (whale meat, see p. 20). This is fried like a steak and, as befits an animal of this size, has a pretty overwhelming taste. Due to its relatively low price, whale meat was once a staple for poor fishing families.

A sumptuous evening meal should be accompanied by wine. Tap water is served with all meals; it is of such high quality that it is even exported. The trademark beverage, however, is coffee. It is the essential conclusion to every meal and a permanent feature of every get-together. In the evening, Icelanders like to pep it up with cognac or a liqueur. Coffee is relatively cheap, especially when you consider that the second cup usually comes free.

Today's Menu

Snacks

HANGIKJÖT
Smoked lamb, sliced and eaten cold on rye pancakes *(flatkökur)*

HARÐFISKUR
Haddock, cod or wolffish, dried in the open air and served with butter

RÚGBRAUÐ
Dark, sweet bread (in some places it's baked in hot springs)

Main courses

PLOKKFÍSKUR
Stew consisting of potatoes, fish and onions

HANGIKJÖT
Smoked lamb cooked with potatoes, béchamel sauce and green peas; traditionally eaten at Christmas

LIFRARPYLSA
Liver sausage made from lamb's liver; together with *blóðmór*, it's one of the family of lamb sausages known as *slátur*

Desserts

SKYR
Cream cheese made from skimmed milk; a popular dessert when served with milk or cream and brown sugar

RABARARI
Rhubarb compote, served on its own or with *skyr* or ice cream

HJÓNBANDSSÆLA
This shortbread-like cake is also called "wedded bliss"

Drinks

BJÓR
Icelandic beer brewed with spring or glacier water

MÝSA
Whey that has separated from *skyr*; a refreshing drink and very healthy

BRENNIVÍN
Icelandic aquavit, nicknamed the "Black Death" because of its label (and knock-out quality!)

SHOPPING

You can't take volcanoes home with you, but you can buy a reminder in the form of a lava candlestick or salt cellar. Or maybe a lava-bead necklace – you'll hardly notice you're wearing it because it is so light. Icelandic design has plenty on offer – sometimes kitschy, sometimes creative, but always typically Icelandic: a tray of Iceland-shaped ice cubes, for example. It's worth a foray into the small shops in Reykjavík city centre to find the best souvenirs.

LAMB & SALMON

If you like Icelandic food, you can try out some recipes at home using Icelandic lamb. Delicious vacuum-packed lamb chops are easy to transport. You can find them in every supermarket, as well as at cooperatives such as in Hvammstangi in the north. Round off your menu with a few slices of salmon. You'll find a large selection of Icelandic foods at the *Icemarket* at the airport.

MUSIC

Icelandic music comes highly recommended. Make sure you listen to the latest albums, from classical through indie rock to techno, from Björk to Bubi Morten. You'll find a fine and up-to-date selection and help on hand to guide you through it at *12 Tónar (Skólavörðustigur 15)* in Reykjavík.

NATURAL BEAUTY

Skincare range *Blue Lagoon* sells healing mud. The products are available in Reykjavík, as well as at the Blue Lagoon geothermal spa. At the *Nature Baths* at Mývatn *(see p. 83)* they also sell their own skincare range based on healing minerals; so far, it's only available on site.

Shops display colourful items to catch your eye

FISHY FASHION

Icelanders are very fashion-conscious, and you can buy all big-name international labels here. Icelandic designer brands, however, are something special. A handbag or wallet made of fish skin is a real eye-catcher, especially if it comes from *Atson (atson.is)*. Some designer shops also sell shoes made from fish skin, but fewer are produced these days.

ONLY IN ICELAND

If you like things a touch more exotic, head for *Spaksmannsspjarir (spaks.is)* for fashions inspired by the Icelandic landscape. Unusual items made from surprising materials are to be found at *Kirsuberjatréð* in Reykjavík's Vesturgata: jewellery made from bits of plastic hosepipe or handknitted oversized jumpers *(kirs.is)*. The Icelandic label *66° North (66north.com)* manufactures excellent outdoor garments from recycled plastic bottles and organic cotton, among other materials.

IN WITH THE OLD

Shop with a clear conscience in one of the country's many second-hand shops. Find unique and select items at *Wasteland (Ingólfsstræti 5)* in Reykjavík, for example.

COSY WOOL

The classic souvenir from Iceland is of course the Iceland sweater. Beautiful, handknitted models can be found at *Víkurprjón* in Vík í Mýrdal *(Austurvegur 20 | tel. 4 87 12 50)*. The current trendy label for woollen goods, including sweaters, blankets and ponchos, is *Farmers Market (farmersmarket.is)* in Reykjavík.

SPORT & ACTIVITIES

The many outdoor activities on offer are an ideal way to get to know and appreciate Iceland's dramatic landscapes. The horse was once the country's most reliable form of transport. Today, Icelanders ride for pleasure, and the favourite pastime of many Reykjavík families is spending Sundays at the riding stables with their horses.

Swimming is a national institution and an essential skill for children to learn. In recent years, hiking and golf have been discovered by an ever-wider audience.

FISHING

Iceland's rivers are famous for their salmon and trout stocks. Luckily, there's no need to spend hours standing around in the water – the trout and char, in particular, are quick to bite. You can easily obtain fishing licences for trout-fishing spots at short notice from farms and petrol stations near the waters. From late May to late August, why not try deep-sea fishing? It's great fun! And there's no shortage of providers along the coastal towns. In the Westfjords, you can get up close and personal with large marine mammals on observation trips *(westtours.is)*.

INSIDER TIP Whale-watching

GLACIER TOURS

Experienced ice-climbers can undertake solo tours across the Langjökull or the Vatnajökull ice caps, but it is still important to get advice from local hiking guides. Even beginners can try ice-climbing. If you are attempting such a tour for the first time, the excursions offered by the Icelandic touring associations are ideal (see Mountaineering, p. 34, for contacts). Another good source of information and tour operator – especially on the

Trek over rugged snow fields into the icy blue on a tour of the Svínafellsjökull glacier

Vatnajökull – is *Icelandic Mountain Guides (Klettagarðar 12 | Reykjavík | tel. 587 9999 | mountainguides.is)*.

GOLF

There are 65 golf courses in the country, and some greens have been intriguingly incorporated into the lava landscape. Most courses are open to foreign visitors for a reasonable green fee. Golf is a sport for all the family in Iceland, so make sure to pack your putters *(golficeland.org)*.

HIKING

The Highlands and the northwest and northeast of Iceland offer hikers solitude and some intense encounters with nature. Some of the trails are well marked and very popular; others you can discover very much alone. The main prerequisite for a multi-day trek is to be in good physical shape and to have the right equipment, as you must reckon on experiencing all kinds of weather. Good hiking maps and guides for the most popular routes are available from most bookshops in Reykjavík. One-day walks, for example on Hekla volcano or around Skaftafell, are also a great way to see the countryside.

Organised tours are offered by the two Icelandic *touring associations* (see Mountaineering, p.34) and *Icelandic Mountain Guides* in Reykjavík (see Glacier Tours, above). Ideal for families are the guided tours by *Wanderlust (wanderlust.is)*, which sometimes come with a picnic. The guided walks in Höfn with tour guide *Hulda* are a very relaxing and intimate experience *(hofnlocalguide.com)*

HORSE RIDING

Horses are very much a part of Iceland, and opportunities for riding are correspondingly plentiful. They range from one-hour rides – including for complete beginners – to Highland tours lasting several weeks, with two horses per rider. *Íshestar* in *Hafnarfjörður* offers short horseback excursions *(tel. 555 7000 | ishestar.is)*. Arinbjörn Jóhannsson at *Brekkulækur Farm (Brekkulækur | tel. 451 2938 | abbi-island.is)* will help you get to know the Arnarvatnsheiði plateau – the ultimate, back-to-nature experience. Other horse-riding stables can be found in the *Hey Iceland* brochure *Self-Drive in Iceland*, where farms with horse-riding facilities are marked *(hey iceland.is)*. Personal riding equipment and clothing must be disinfected before entering the country!

KAYAK

Experienced kayakers can explore a lot of Iceland from the water. Kayak tours into the fjords or on the Heinabergslón glacier lagoon are spectacular, and both can be done in summer. You can silently cut through the waters to the icebergs *(iceguide.is/tours)*.

INSIDER TIP
Kayak on a glacier lagoon

LONG-DISTANCE RUNNING

Iceland offers some fantastic routes for long-distance runners. The Reykjavík Marathon takes place every year around 20 August. The classic 55km hiking route from Landmannalaugar to Þórsmörk is used for the Laugevegur Ultra Marathon. The Suzuki Midnight Sun Run held in Reykjavík in June offers participants the opportunity to choose one of three different distances: a half-marathon, 10km and 5km; but you can also register to take part in all three distances. At the end of May/ beginning of June is the Mývatn Marathon. Information on all races: *reykjaviksport.is*

MOUNTAIN BIKING

If you couldn't bring your mountain bike with you, you can hire one in Reykjavík and a number of other towns and villages. The routes along the coast near Reykjavík or around the Mývatn Lake are beautiful and ideal for hobby cyclists. Tourist information offices have lists of places to hire mountain bikes and book guided tours. Information: *Icelandic Mountain Bike Club (fjallahjolak lubburinn.is)*.

MOUNTAINEERING

The country's many mountains are an open invitation to climbing enthusiasts, but the prevalence of loose surface rock and sudden changes in the weather mean that individual tours are only to be recommended for experienced mountaineers. Essential equipment on any mountain excursion should include emergency rations and a first-aid kit, plus a bivouac sack and emergency foil blanket. Two Icelandic touring associations also offer guided tours. Both have their headquarters in Reykjavík: *Ferðafélag Íslands (Mörkin 6 | tel. 568 2533 | fi.is); Útivist (Katrínartúni 4 | tel. 562 1000 | utivist.is)*.

RAFTING

Fun for all the family at several locations on the larger glacial rivers.

Riding at Húsavík is a fun family activity

Operators include *Arctic Rafting (Drumboddsstaðir River Base | Selfoss | tel. 486 8990 | arcticrafting.is)* in the south and, in Sveitarfélagið, *Viking Rafting (tel. 823 8300 | vikingrafting.is)*.

STAND-UP PADDLING

A sport made for Iceland! A popular spot for paddling is Iceland's largest lake, þingvallavatn. Another lake suitable for SUP is Hvalfjörður. Tour company *adventurevikings.is* provides a stand-up paddleboard and all the gear for paddling here.

SWIMMING

Swimming is the national sport. Once you've tried the warm waters of the open-air swimming pools, you're sure to be hooked. In Reykjavík alone there are seven pools, and several more in the surrounding villages where, in particular, efforts have been made to upgrade facilities, making these the ideal spot for a family day out. Every large town or village has an open-air swimming pool.

WINTER SPORTS

Why not indulge in some winter sports in Iceland? There are excellent ski resorts, for example, above Akureyri on *Hlíðarfjall*. Snow conditions permitting, you can take attractive cross-country tours all over the island; the Icelanders' favourite places are the northwest and Mývatn areas. In addition, you could try one of the Ski-Doo snowmobile tours on signposted routes.

REGIONAL OVERVIEW

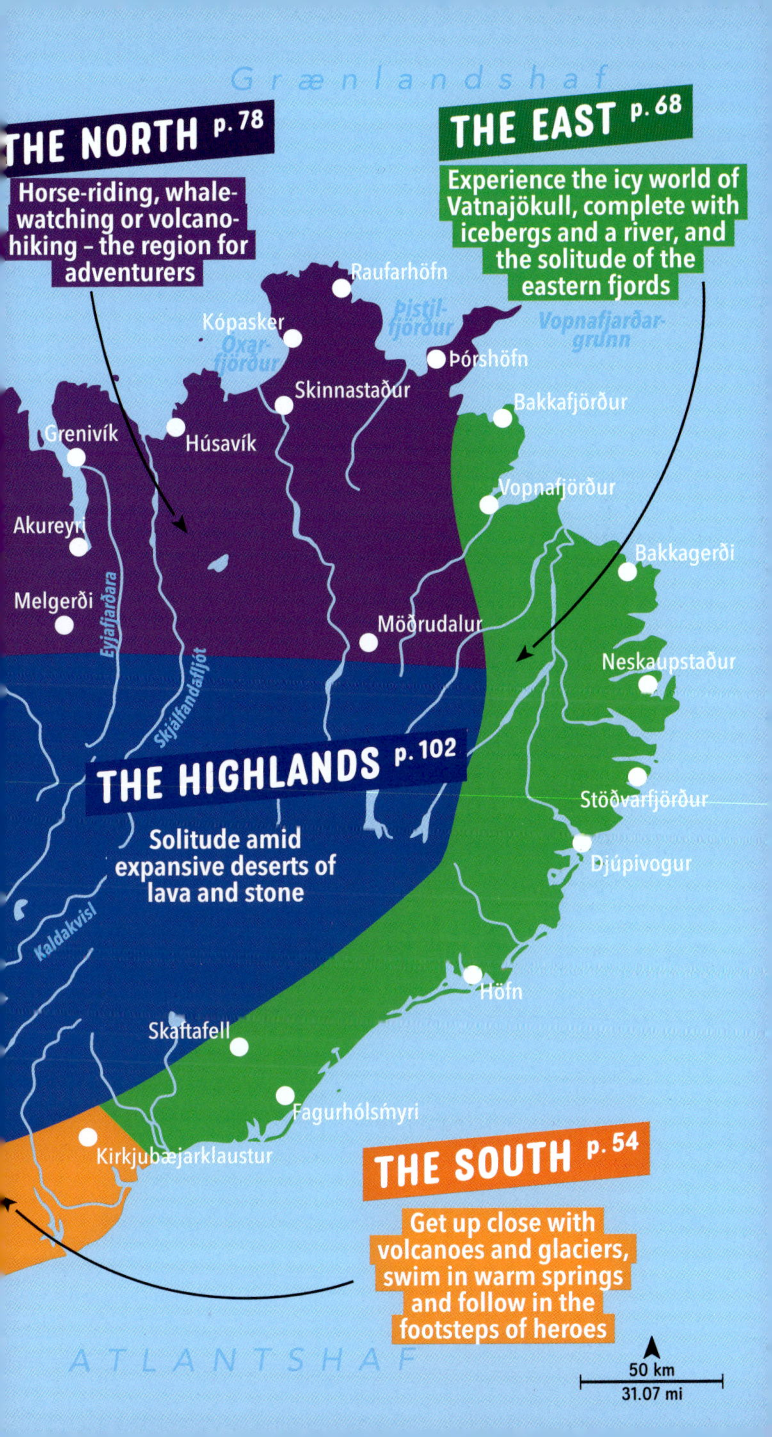

Grænlandshaf
THE NORTH p. 78
Horse-riding, whale-watching or volcano-hiking – the region for adventurers
THE EAST p. 68
Experience the icy world of Vatnajökull, complete with icebergs and a river, and the solitude of the eastern fjords
Raufarhöfn
Kópasker
Þistilfjörður
Oxarfjörður
Vopnafjarðargrunn
Þórshöfn
Skinnastaður
Bakkafjörður
Grenivík
Húsavík
Vopnafjörður
Akureyri
Bakkagerði
Melgerði
Eyjafjarðara
Möðrudalur
Skjálfandafljót
Neskaupstaður
THE HIGHLANDS p. 102
Stöðvarfjörður
Solitude amid expansive deserts of lava and stone
Djúpivogur
Kaldakvísl
Höfn
Skaftafell
Fagurhólsmýri
Kirkjubæjarklaustur
THE SOUTH p. 54
Get up close with volcanoes and glaciers, swim in warm springs and follow in the footsteps of heroes
ATLANTSHAF
50 km
31.07 mi

REYKJAVÍK

COOL AND CREATIVE

Reykjavík (pop. 135,700) is modern and dynamic, yet with the charm of a village. The best views over the city and its surroundings are from the tower of the Hallgrímskirkja or the Perlan glass dome. Enjoy the colourful houses in the city centre, the villa districts with their beautiful gardens in the centre and west, and the stylish new apartment blocks: it's chic urban life on the coast.

Reykjavík is the economic, political and cultural heart of the country. Founded just 250 years ago, the city is bursting with life and exciting

The Harpa Concert Hall and Conference Centre resembles giant ice cubes

places to discover. A UNESCO City of Literature, it is also home to countless galleries exhibiting works – often by young artists – in the small side streets of Laugavegur. Designer shops flourish and a lively café and bar scene offers plenty of scope for enjoyment. Reykjavík invites you to explore it in all its diversity, from art, entertainment and partying to sunsets and the Northern Lights; from hot dogs to gourmet menus; from small alleyways to expansive parks. And not far away are thrilling natural wonders in the midst of a lava landscape.

REYKJAVÍK

MARCO POLO HIGHLIGHTS

★ **HAFNARHÚS (HARBOUR HOUSE)**
Beautifully displayed works by Icelandic artist Erró ➤ p. 43

★ **HARPA**
Shimmering conference and concert hall ➤ p. 44

★ **HALLGRÍMSKIRKJA**
Reykjavík's landmark church, with a 76m-high tower ➤ p. 45

★ **PERLAN**
Futuristic glass dome atop six huge hot-water tanks ➤ p. 47

★ **ÞINGVELLIR**
Iceland's most important historic location is also a geological highlight ➤ p. 52

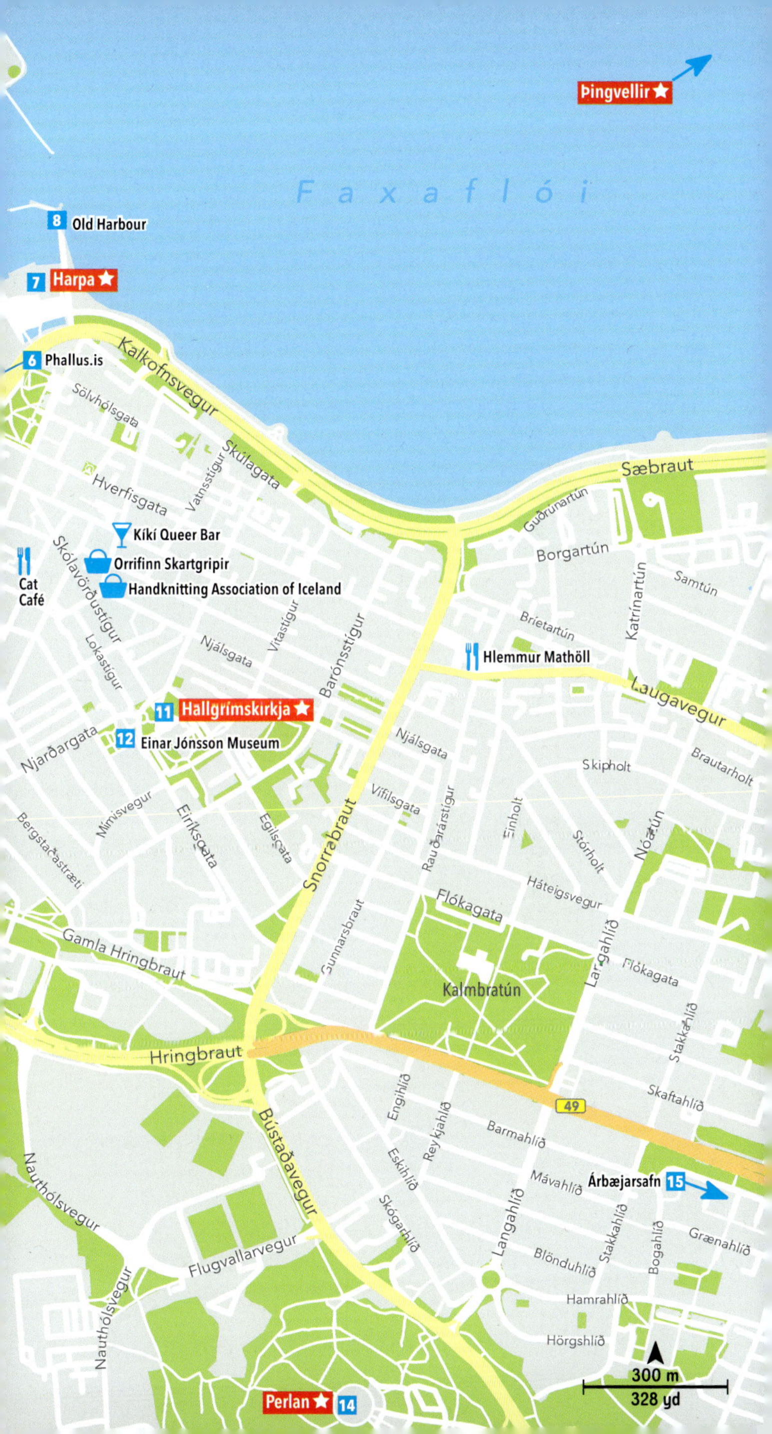
Þingvellir
Faxaflói
8 Old Harbour
7 Harpa
6 Phallus.is
Kalkofnsvegur
Sölvhólsgata
Skúlagata
Vatnsstígur
Hverfisgata
Kíkí Queer Bar
Orrifinn Skartgripir
Handknitting Association of Iceland
Cat Café
Skólavörðustígur
Lokastígur
Njálsgata
Vitastígur
Barónsstígur
Sæbraut
Guðrúnartún
Borgartún
Samtún
Katrínartún
Bríetartún
Hlemmur Mathöll
Laugavegur
11 Hallgrímskirkja
12 Einar Jónsson Museum
Njarðargata
Njálsgata
Skipholt
Brautarholt
Vífilsgata
Mímisvegur
Eiríksgata
Egilsgata
Snorrabraut
Rauðarárstígur
Einholt
Stórholt
Nóatún
Bergstaðastræti
Háteigsvegur
Flókagata
Gamla Hringbraut
Gunnarsbraut
Lönguhlíð
Flókagata
Kalmbratún
Stakkahlíð
Hringbraut
Engihlíð
Reykjahlíð
49
Skaftahlíð
Barmahlíð
Bústaðavegur
Eskihlíð
Mávahlíð
Árbæjarsafn 15
Nauthólsvegur
Skógarhlíð
Langahlíð
Stakkahlíð
Bogahlíð
Grænahlíð
Flugvallarvegur
Blönduhlíð
Hamrahlíð
Nauthólsvegur
Hörgshlíð
300 m
328 yd
Perlan 14

SIGHTSEEING

1 TJÖRNIN

The northern banks of Lake Tjörnin (locally called "the Pond"), are a hive of activity and popular with locals and children. At the heart of the city, the lake echoes with the honks and squawks of more than 40 species of visiting birds, including ducks, geese, swans and different types of gull. Farmhouses once lined the southern banks but today the lake is surrounded by green spaces and there are paths around the perimeter. In summer, the lake is a hotspot for locals who come to enjoy a picnic lunch. Why not join them? Grab a delicious salad or snack, take a seat on the grass and enjoy lunch al fresco in true relaxed Icelandic style! *b3*

2 CITY HALL

You'd be forgiven for thinking the City Hall looks as if it's standing in the middle of the lake: a corner of Lake Tjörnin was specially drained to make way for this real architectural eye-catcher, built in 1992. It's structure and location initially earned much criticism from the population – the building detracted from the pretty row of villas which lined the lake shore. Today, though, City Hall is a popular venue for receptions and exhibitions. It is also home of the tourist information centre. The large 3D representation of Iceland will help you with your planning, too. *b3*

WHERE TO START?

The tourist centre is the old part of the city between Lake Tjörnin and the harbour. The central bus station, Lækjartorg, is here. City Hall, with an underground car park, is nearby, as is **Austurvöllur** *(b3)* square, with the Parliament building, Hotel Borg, the cathedral and cafés. From here, head for Harbour House and the shopping street Laugavegur.

3 AUSTURVÖLLUR

This is where the people of Iceland make their voice heard. It's the site of all political rallies, which is why this square in front of the parliament building is so well known. In its centre is a *statue of Iceland's national hero Jón Sigurðsson*, crafted by Einar Jónsson. He looks towards a grey basalt building: the seat of the Icelandic parliament, the *Alþingishús*. It was built in 1881 and an extension was added in 2001. To the left of this stands Reykjavík's oldest church, *Dómkirkja*, dating from 1776. The eastern side of the square is dominated by the venerable *Hótel Borg*, opened in 1930. In summer the square is a favourite spot for having fun. *b3*

4 AÐALSTRÆTI

Visiting Reykjavík's oldest street is like stepping back in time. Starting at its southern end, the foundations of a Viking longhouse from the tenth century can be viewed at *The Settlement Exhibition (daily 10am–5pm | admission 2500 ISK, free for children; also valid for Aðalstræti 10 |*

Worship in Reykjavík's oldest church or demonstrate in front of the parliament building

reykjavikcitymuseum.is). They date from the time of Iceland's first settlers and could even have been part of the home of Ingólfur Arnarson, the first permanent Norse settler – a nice idea at least! The artefacts on display are part of a captivating multimedia exhibition on the settlement of the area.

The square opposite holds a statue of Skúli Magnússon (1711–1794). He founded Iceland's first wool factory in *Aðalstræti no. 10*, thus laying the foundation for Reykjavík's prominence as a trading centre. The cottage-like building is still standing. Today, there are two exhibitions focusing on Iceland's history *(daily 10am–5pm)*. At the end of the street stands a replica 18th-century warehouse from which a tunnel once led to the harbour. It was largely used to smuggle gyrfalcons, kept in the warehouse, to the ships waiting in the harbour to take them to their aristocratic European buyers. *b3*

5 HAFNARHÚS (HARBOUR HOUSE) ★

The former warehouse on the harbour is ideal for events of all kinds, and the works on display by Icelandic artist Erro are quite something. Born Guðmundur Guðmundsson, this visual artist created around 4,000 works of art and most of them can be seen here. His large-scale paintings are in the style of pop art and borrow heavily from comics, both witty and political. Mickey Mouse and Lenin send their regards. The café has views over the harbour. *Daily 10am–5pm (Thu until 10pm) | admission 1,950 ISK | Tryggvagata | artmuseum.isv | b3*

6 PHALLUS.IS

One of a kind ... Penises from all species of mammal – and since 2011 even from a human being – are on display here. The museum also has a number of penis curiosities and artistic works from around the world. *Daily 10am–7pm | admission 2,500 ISK | Hafnartorg | phallus.is | b3*

7 HARPA ★

Approaching Reykjavík from the sea, you can't fail to notice the multistorey, multicoloured glass building on the harbour. The Harpa Concert Hall and Conference Centre has a stunning glass façade by artist Olafur Elíasson. Once inside, the honeycomb windows form beautiful lines. The absolute highlight is the window lighting, which can be synchronised to music. In addition to event venues, the building houses a number of shops and bars, as well as the Icelandic pavilion from the 2010 World's Fair that shows a 15-minute film about Iceland on a 360° screen. *Austurbakki 2 | harpa.is | toilets 300 ISK (in summer) | c2–3*

REYKJAVÍK CITY CARD

Whatever you do, make sure to pick up a *Reykjavík City Card*, which comes with options of one day (4,400 ISK), two days (6,120 ISK) or three days (7,520 ISK). The cards are valid for those aged 18 and over and include unlimited public transport within the city, free entry to eight museums and the Árbærsafn open-air museum, seven municipal swimming pools, the ice rink and Family Park and Zoo (in summer), a boat trip to Viðeyund, and so much more. You can pick up a card at the Tourist Information Centre, some museums and hotels, and main bus stations. Alternatively, get one online at *visitreykjavik.is/city-card/front*. You'll need to print it out.

8 OLD HARBOUR

Once the flourishing hub of the fishing and marine industry, most of the shipping companies have now left and the buildings have been transformed into designer boutiques, restaurants, cafés, galleries and museums. The trendy new district stretches from the Örfirisey peninsula in the west to the docking points for smaller cruise ships close to Harpa. The best way to explore the area is by bike or even Segway. Reykjavík's best ice-cream is served at *Valdís*, where you can try an Icelandic speciality, liquorice ice-cream. Once a herring factory and warehouse, the Marshall House is now home to a cutting-edge museum for contemporary art, *Nýlistasafn (Wed–Sun noon–6pm | free admission | nylo.is)*. The avant-garde *Kling & Bang* gallery is also based here, as well as the studio of the internationally acclaimed Icelandic artist *Ólafur Elíasson*. Every street in the area is worth a peep and photographers will fall in love with the view of Reykjavík from here: it is transformed into a "real" city with a skyline. Amid the design and art, you can still find tradition, with old fishing pubs and small fishing boats that sell the catch of the day to the chefs at gourmet restaurants.

Grandagarður Street leads you to the Örfiresey peninsula. Do not let the large warehouses distort your impression – behind the façade, you'll find small enterprises with factory outlets such as chocolatier *OmNom (daily 1–10pm | Hólmaslóð 4 | omnom chocolate.com)*, which uses extremely high-quality cocoa beans roasted with nuts in a 50:50 ratio to produce their sumptuous chocolate. As well as chocolate, you can buy delicious ice cream topped with their signature wolf image and other tasty chocolate-related creations. *a–b 1–2*

INSIDER TIP
Scream for ice cream!

9 AURORA BOREALIS

Lose yourself in the magic world of the Northern Lights as they sway and dance all around you. This museum explains the phenomenon, complete with photo footage – an ideal stop if you have not yet seen this natural wonder in real life. The shop sells T-shirts in Northern Lights colours. *Daily 9am–9pm | admission 2,000 ISK | Grandagarður 2 | aurorareykjavik.is | a2*

10 VÍKIN – MARITIME MUSEUM (SJÓMINJASAFN)

Fishing belongs to Iceland just as much as volcanoes, and this museum provides an insight into the history and lives of fishermen. Rather fittingly, today's museum is housed in a former cold store. The coastguard vessel *Óðinn*, which once served in the Cod Wars, when Icelanders fought for their 200-mile exclusion zone, is docked at the entrance. It has a shop and a restaurant with a waterside patio. *Daily 10am–5pm | guided tour of ship 11am, 1pm, 2pm, 3pm | admission 1,950 ISK,*

Fishing boats have been replaced by cafés and galleries at the Old Harbour

Óðinn 1,500 ISK, joint ticket 3,000 ISK | Grandagarður 8 | borgarsogusafn.is/en/reykjavik-maritime-museum | b2

11 HALLGRÍMSKIRKJA ★

You can spot the 76m-high tower of this modern church from far away; it was named after the author of *Passion Hymns*, Hallgrímur Pétursson (1614–74). Head for the church from Skólavörðustígur and it looks like the building is just waiting to greet you. Built to a highly unconventional design by Guðjon Samúelsson, it can accommodate 1,200 worshippers. The architect took his inspiration from the vertical arrangement of basalt columns when designing the sweeping tower façade. Construction took over 40 years, and the church was finally consecrated in 1986; the huge organ was added in 1992. Regular *organ concerts* are staged during the summer months – a real acoustic treat in these bright, generously proportioned surroundings. A statue of Leifur Eiríksson, the man who "discovered" the New World, stands in front of the church. The sculpture by Stirling Calder was a gift from the USA in 1930 (to celebrate 1,000 years of the Alþing) and echoes the shape of the tower. *Tower: daily 10am–7.30pm | trip up the tower 1,200 ISK | Hallgrímstorg 1 | hallgrimskirkja.is | c4*

12 EINAR JÓNSSON MUSEUM

The former home and studio of sculptor and painter Einar Jónsson (1874–1954) is now a museum. Jónsson has become a somewhat controversial figure in Iceland, with his heroic-style sculptures of Norse figures attracting appreciation from white supremacists. However, almost every influential Icelander was cast in bronze by Jónsson. The sculpture garden behind the museum is also well worth a visit. *Tue–Sun noon–5pm | admission 1,500 ISK | Eíriksgata 3 | lej.is | Garden open all year round | free admission | c4*

13 ICELANDIC NATIONAL MUSEUM (ÞJÓÐMINJASAFN)

Explore the history and culture of Iceland. Playful exhibits use

The spectacular Northern Lights even outshine Hallgrímskirkja

multimedia to introduce visitors to the lives of Icelanders from the first settlers to the present day. There are also changing exhibitions. The success of the exhibits and the bright architecture of the rooms have earned the museum an award; there's also a good shop and café! *May–15 Sept daily 10am–5pm, 16 Sept–April Tue–Sun 10am–5pm | admission 2,500 ISK | Suðurgata 41 | thjodminjasafn.is | 1 hr | b4*

14 PERLAN ★

Perlan ("The Pearl") is the futuristic landmark of Reykjavík and crowns the top of the wooded Öskjuhlíð hill. This mirrored glass dome, in which the sun, clouds and the sky are all reflected, is built on top of six huge hot-water tanks. The tanks once stored up to 20m litres of geothermal water from the Reykjavík region to heat homes, swimming pools and pavements. Today, only two of the tanks are still in operation, while the others house the *Wonders of Iceland* exhibition, which takes you inside a chilly artificial glacier cave for an interactive glacier exploration, allows you to experience the magic of the Northern Lights, or stroll through land and sea and gaze at the stars. This sensational exhibition is ideal for families. There is a 360° viewing deck around the mirrored dome from where you can enjoy a panoramic view to the Snæfellsjökull glacier. In addition, a zip line zooms at speeds of 50kmh from Perlan for 230m into woodland. *Daily 9am–7pm | admission 4,690 ISK, children 2,690 ISK | perlan.is | 1–2 hrs | d6*

15 ÁRBÆJARSAFN

How tranquil and rural Reykjavík once was! This open-air museum features 27 traditional buildings dating to the period from 1820 to 1907. There are special programmes for children at weekends and you can take part in courses to learn about old agricultural methods. The exhibition on old toys is also interesting, and there's plenty for "big kids" too, such as four-horned sheep. *Daily June–Aug 10am–5pm, Sept–May 1–5pm, guided tours 1pm (in English) | admission 1,740 ISK, free for children | Kistuhylur 4 | reykjavikcitymuseum.is | 0*

EATING & DRINKING

BÆJARINS BEZTU

A real hit with hot dog lovers. Reykjavík locals have been queueing here for generations for the best hot dogs in town. *Daily | corner of Tryggvagata/Pósthússtræti | £ | b3*

CAT CAFÉ

The concept has finally made it to Reykjavík: Iceland's first cat café. Sure to be a hit with any cat lover, with a cosy atmosphere that makes both cats and visitors feel right at home. Cake and coffee are also available, of course! *Daily 11am–5.30pm | Bergstaðastræti 10a | kattakaffihusid.is | £ | c3*

HLEMMUR MATHÖLL

This former bus terminal is now a popular food court with ten different restaurants, bistros and cafés serving diverse cuisines from Asian to vegetarian. It's a great place to kick off your evening. You can buy good bread and Icelandic vegetables here, too, useful if you're self-catering. *Daily 10am–11pm | Laugavegur 107 | hlemmur matholl.is | £–££ | 🕮 d4*

KAFFIVAGNINN

Savour good-quality fish dishes while overlooking the harbour. This is where the fishermen come to eat, too (and have done since 1935). Classic and simple. How about a good old crab sandwich? *Mon–Fri 7.30am–6pm, Sat/Sun 8am–6pm | Grandagarður 10 | tel. 551 5932 | £ | 🕮 b2*

MATARKJALLARINN – FOOD CELLAR

Excellent cuisine made with real Icelandic ingredients such as lamb, fish and herbs. Round off your meal with a cocktail in the piano bar. *Daily 5–11pm, Mon–Fri also 11.30am–2.30pm | Aðalstræti 2 | tel. 558 0000 | £££ | 🕮 b3*

SHOPPING

The main shopping streets in Reykjavík are *Laugavegur*, *Aðalstræti* and *Skólavörðurstigur*. As well as an excellent selection of designer and fashion shops, you will also find plenty of innovative jewellers.

INSIDER TIP Browse for books

Hoping for the latest thriller? A chic coffee table volume? Don't miss the *Eymundsson* bookshop.

For a treat for your ears, try the stores *Skifan* and *12 Tónar*. Here, you'll find the hottest sounds Iceland's music business has to offer. There are a range of Icelandic and international outlets, as well as cafés and cinemas, in the *Kringlan* and *Smáralind* (just outside Kópavogur) shopping malls. At the *Kolaportið flea market* on the harbour, you're bound to discover stuff you never knew you needed *(Sat/Sun 11am–5pm)*.

HANDKNITTING ASSOCIATION OF ICELAND

How about something knitted? A wide range of handmade hats, sweaters and blankets from traditional to fashionable are sold at this knitting collective. You can also buy Icelandic yarn and knitting patterns and do it yourself. *Mon–Fri 9am–6pm, Sat/Sun noon–6pm | Skólavörðustígur 19 | tel. 552 1890 | handknit.is | 🕮 c3*

ORRIFINN SKARTGRIPIR

On the hunt for that special piece of jewellery from Iceland? You might just find it in this workshop, for example braided bracelets and rings made from both silver and bronze. *Mon–Fri 10am–6pm, Sat 11am–4pm | Skólavörðustíg 43 | tel. 789 7616 | orrifinn.com | 🕮 c4*

SPORT & ACTIVITIES

BIKE & SEGWAY

You can explore the city on your own by bike, including by electric bike, or join a guided tour by bike or Segway with *Reykjavík Bike Tours (summer daily from 9am, winter Fri/Sat from 10am | Ægisgarður 7, at the Old Harbour | tel. 694 8956 | icelandbike.com)*. The route along the coast as far

You're sure to find something to buy on Laugavegur

as the bird sanctuary at the Grótta Lighthouse is ideal for an excursion by bike. Bike hire is also available at *Borgarhjól (Hverfisgata 50 | tel. 551 5653 | c3)*.

DIVING

You can go on diving trips around Reykjavík, on the Reykjanes peninsula and in Þingvallavatn. Night dives as well as snorkelling are also available *Dive Iceland | Hátún 15 | tel. 888 8080 | diveiceland.com*

BEACHES

NAUTHÓLSVÍK

Yes, Reykjavík does have its own beach, on the edge of the Öskjuhlíð recreational area. And thanks to the hot spring, you can enjoy a water temperature of 20°C. In summer, it's heaving with sunbathers as the entire beach is just 100m long – but it's a special place nonetheless. *15 May–15 Aug daily 10am–7pm, 16 Aug–14 May Mon, Wed 11am–2pm, 5–8pm, Tue, Thu 11am–2pm, Sat 11am–4pm | winter 740 ISK, free in summer | Nauthólsvegur | nautholsvik.is | 0*

WELLNESS

Home to eight thermal spas (*Laugardalur* is the biggest), Reykjavík is also known as Spa City. If you just want to relax, head for *Vesturbæjarlaug (a3) (Hofsvallagata | admission 1,100 ISK)*: this is where the city's rich and famous meet up.

INSIDER TIP **Relax with the locals**

Or bathe among locals away from the tourist trail at the *Grafarvógslaug* thermal pool *(Dalhús, Grafarvógur | admission 1,100 ISK)*. Right next door to the large Laugardal spa in Reykjavík is the spa resort of *Laugar (f3) (Sundlaugavegi 30a |*

admission from 6,500 ISK | laugarspa.com), with its wide range of wellness treatments (hot water and cosmetic treatments, plus massages).

NIGHTLIFE

KÍKÍ QUEER BAR

The meeting place for the queer scene or just anyone looking for a good night out. Spanning two floors, this bar has always been popular, whatever name it's currently using. *Laugavegur 22 | kiki.is | 🕮 c3*

SIRKUS

One of the city's most legendary spots is back. Full of art – around 20 different artists exhibit here – and music, it's the ideal place to enjoy a cocktail. *Lækjargata 6 | tel. 696 8163 | 🕮 b3*

SLIPPBARINN

A favourite spot among the locals, with music on Wednesdays as well as other events. A great place to hang out and enjoy breakfast, brunch or dinner. *Myrargata 2 | tel. 560 8080 | slippbarinn.is | 🕮 b2*

AROUND REYKJAVÍK

GRÓTTA LIGHTHOUSE

10km west of Reykjavík, the most scenic route is by bike

The Grótta Lighthouse sits at the furthermost tip of the *Seltjarnarnes* peninsula – a real spot for lovers. Young Icelanders used to come here in summer and winter alike, and it's not unusual for coachloads of visitors to turn up in the hope of seeing the Northern Lights. You'll struggle to find a better view out over the sea at sunset in Reykjavík – you can see as far as Snæfellsjökull when the skies are clear. When the tide is out, you can easily walk to the lighthouse from the beach. A lovely footpath along the coast leads to this spot, and there's an official bird sanctuary not far from the beach. *🕮 E9*

VIÐEY

1km from Skarfabakki harbour, Reykjavík, by ferry

The little island in the Kollafjörður fjord to the north of the city is a charming place for a day trip. Evidence of its long history can be seen in the oldest surviving building in the country, constructed from 1753 to 1755 by governor Skúli Magnússon. The tiny church next door dates back to 1774. The signposted footpaths on the island lead you eastwards to the ruins of a village that boasted an international port until the beginning of the 20th century. The west of the island is the setting for Richard Serra's ensemble of standing stones, *Afangar*, or "Stages", which harmonises perfectly with the landscape, with Reykjavík in the background. Back in 2007, Yoko Ono had the Image Peace Tower erected on Viðey in memory of her husband John Lennon. *Ferry daily hourly 10.15am–5.15pm, from Viðey 10.30am–6.30pm | 1,950 ISK | 🕮 E9*

HAFNARFJÖRÐUR

12km south of Reykjavík, 15 mins by car or 20 mins by bus

Hafnafjörður's excellent harbour made it an important trading post and the main port of the German Hanseatic League in Iceland. The harbour remains a major commercial centre, not least because of the nearby Straumsvík aluminium smelting plant.

Fancy meeting a few elves and Vikings? Then Hafnafjörður is the place for you. The town was built in the *Búrfellshraun* lava field, which defines its character. It is said that huge elf colonies are hidden in the lava formations, and you can even take a walk through the imaginary dwellings of the fairy folk *(Tourist Information Office | tel. 585 5500)*. The Vikings, too, felt at home here. Every year, there is a Viking Festival with a medieval market. *Víðistaðatún Park* is a great place to stop and enjoy the grilled lamb. *E9–10*

ÞRÍHNÚKAGÍGUR

34km southeast of Reykjavík along the 417, 20 mins by car; shuttle service from Reykjavík

INSIDER TIP **Journey into a volcano**

The tour takes you some 120m inside the Þríhnúkagígur volcano, which has been inactive for the last 4,000 years. The entrance to this unique experience starts near the Blafjöll ski resort. *44,000 ISK | tel. 519 5609 | insidethevolcano.com |* *E10*

BLÁA LÓNIÐ (BLUE LAGOON)

40km southwest of Reykjavík, 45 mins by car, regular bus connections

The most famous pool in Iceland lies,

The Blue Lagoon is particularly atmospheric in the winter

encircled by a landscape of lava, on the Reykjanes peninsula. The water comes from the geothermal power plant nearby; in other words, it's wastewater. This clever marketing strategy attracts thousands of visitors each year. The cloudy blue lake gets its colour from the minerals and algae it contains, which have proven healing properties in the treatment of skin conditions. Bathing in the warm water (38°C), full of salts and minerals, is relaxing for body and mind, and a peeling with a silica mud mask is a great way to thoroughly cleanse your skin. Other spa offerings include massages and facial treatments. The spa's *restaurant (tel. 420 8800 | ££–£££)* serves everything from light dishes to gourmet menus. Very crowded in summer! *From 8,490 ISK: timed tickets must be purchased online in advance | 240 Grindavík | tel. 420 8800 | bluelagoon.com |* *D10*

ÞINGVELLIR ★

45km east of Reykjavík, 50 mins by car or 1 hr by bus

Þingvellir translates as "Parliament Plains" and it is where the most historically significant events in Icelandic history have taken place, from the declaration of the free state in 930 to the founding of the Republic of Iceland in 1944. Icelanders regard the site as central to their national identity. It became a national park in 1928 and a UNESCO World Heritage Site in

2004. It was chosen as the location for the original Alþing (parliament) for its size, accessibility by the settlers, and the presence of water and grazing areas for their horses. Once a year, the different *goðar* (leaders) and their free farmers would meet for a period of 14 days to hear laws, pass judgements and make political decisions.

From the observation point, with adjoining *information centre (daily 9am–7pm | toilets 200 ISK, parking 750 ISK, pay online at checkit.is | thing vellir.is)*, you have a fine view across the landscape, including Iceland's largest lake, *Þingvallavatn* (85km²), the mountains surrounding it, plus the *Almannagjá* ("Everyman's Ravine") and the track that runs through it. From the *Lögberg* ("Law Rock"), the speaker recited the laws; former execution sites are located close by. To the north of the Almannagjá is the *Öxarárfoss* waterfall, which was artificially constructed, presumably in the tenth century, to allow the waters of the Öxará to flow into the plain and to the horses.

In geological terms, too, Þingvellir is highly significant. It is a continuation of the Mid-Atlantic Ridge, where the Eurasian and North American plates are still drifting apart, as demonstrated by the two ravines, *Almannagjá* and *Hrafnagjá* ("Raven's Ravine"), running from the northeast to the southwest. Measurements have shown that Þingvellir is sinking by 8mm and widening by 2cm every year.

For divers, the descent into the Silfra Rift between the continental plates to a depth of almost 15m is a memorable experience. There are even night dives on offer *(diveiceland.com)*. 🕮 F9

WHERE TO SLEEP IN REYKJAVÍK

LIVING HISTORY

Successful wrestler Jóhannes frá Borg used the prize money he had won in the US to build his hotel. Located right on the *Austurvöllur* (🕮 b3), the landmark Hotel Borg is a luxury establishment, decorated with memorabilia from Jóhannes as well as from its wild era during the 1950s, when it housed a dance-hall. *56 rooms | Pósthússtræti 11 | tel. 551 1440 | hotelborg.is | £££*

THE SOUTH

HOT SPRINGS AND ACTIVE VOLCANOES

The countryside in the south is picture-postcard stuff, with green meadows and pastures, and broad, black sandy beaches. Further east, these give way to outwash plains, formed by melt-water deposits from the foot of the Mýrdalsjökull glacier.

This is one of country's the most active volcano zones, with frequent eruptions and earthquakes. Hekla, once believed to be the gateway to Hell, hisses regularly, and eruptions of sub-glacial volcanoes, such as Eyjafjallajökull in 2010, are particularly dangerous.

Gullfoss is also known as the "golden waterfall"

This one not only caused devastating flooding, but also threw up an ash cloud that brought worldwide air traffic to a standstill. In 2023, it was the turn of Fagradalsfjall, near Grindavík; and in 2024, crater rows in Reykjanes were erupting.

The geothermal energy in the south is used to heat the region's many greenhouses and to generate electricity; you can also get an idea of its power at the famous geyser in Haukadalur – a real water show.

THE SOUTH

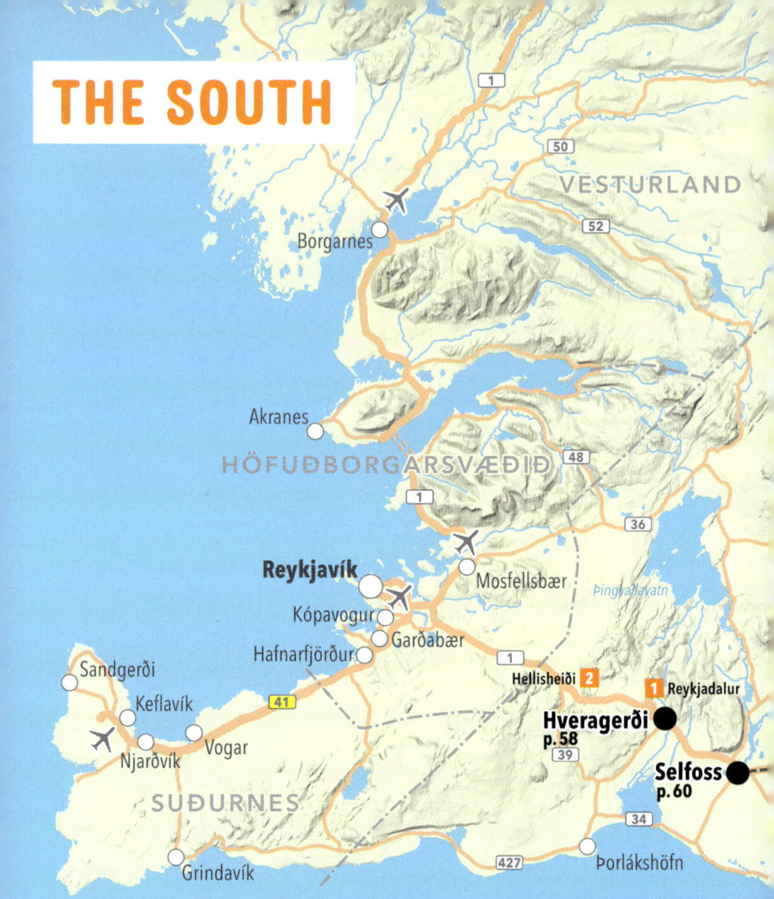

MARCO POLO HIGHLIGHTS

★ **GEYSIR**
The one that gave its name to all the others ➤ p. 61

★ **GULLFOSS**
The sheer beauty of a stunningly powerful waterfall ➤ p. 61

★ **ÞÓRSMÖRK**
"Thor's Forest" lies protected by glaciers ➤ p. 62

★ **HEKLA**
Once thought to be a gateway to Hell, and still an active volcano ➤ p. 63

★ **HEIMAEY**
A single island with double peaks ➤ p. 63

Geysir
4
5
Gullfoss
SUÐURLAND
Reykholt
3
72km, 1 hr
30
26
9
Hekla
50km, 1½ hrs
1
Hvolsvöllur
p. 61
6
Illíðarendi
8
Þórsmörk
7
Seljalandsfoss
33km, 25 mins
1
11
Skógar
Vestmannaeyjabær
Heimaey
p. 63
Vík í Mýrdal
p. 66
Dyrhólaey
10
20 km
12.43 mi

HVERAGERÐI

(🕮 F10) **Its sheltered location in a valley and its thermal springs have allowed Hveragerði to become Iceland's market garden.**

Numerous greenhouses provide warmth and shelter for vegetable growing. The town is also the location of the state-run Horticultural College, with its experimental gardens and research departments. Tourism is another important economic factor, as is healthcare, with a rehabilitation facility for rheumatism sufferers and a centre run by the Icelandic Naturopathic Medical Association. More and more artists have also relocated here in recent years, giving Hveragerdi a reputation as a "hippie village".

SIGHTSEEING

THE QUAKE

This exhibit in the *Sunnumörk* shopping centre shows the aftermath of the May 2008 earthquake. The exhibition includes objects that were destroyed during the quake, which reached 6.3 on the Richter scale. You can also experience how an earthquake feels in a simulator (700 ISK). *Sunnumörk 2–4 | free admission*

THERMAL AREA 🐷

One of the town's many thermal areas is situated right in the centre of town. Here you can find out more about the different springs, their uses and geological structure. *June–Aug Mon–Sat 9am–6pm, Sun 10am–4pm, call for additional opening hours | admission 300 ISK, children free | Hveramörk 13 | tel. 483 5062*

EATING & DRINKING

RESTAURANT VARMÁ

Slow food with a view of the river and excellent dishes made from Icelandic products, such as cod or foal. *Daily 8am–10pm | Hverhamar | tel. 483 4959 | ££–£££*

SPORT & ACTIVITIES

You can sign up for riding excursions of various lengths, including beginners' courses with Icelandic horses for kids, with *Elðhestar (Vellir | tel. 480 4800 | eldhestar.is)*. The adventure of rounding up sheep at the end of summer is a fantastic experience for experienced riders.

Sundlaugin Laugaskarði is not just one of Iceland's prettiest pools, but one of its oldest too. Alongside stylish architecture and relaxing atmosphere, it also boasts a 50m pool, hot pots, plus sunbeds and a sauna. *15 May–14 Sep Mon–Fri 6.45am–9.30pm, Sat/Sun 10am–7pm, 15 Sep–14 May Mon–Fri 6.45am–8.30pm, Sat/Sun 10am–5.15pm | 1,000 ISK | Reykjamörk | tel. 483 4113*

WELLNESS

HEILSUSTOFNUN NLFÍ

Although its main function is as a rehab centre, this facility also offers treatments for everyone, including mud baths, soothing massages and herbal

Greenhouses at Hveragerði provide warmth and shelter for vegetables to grow

baths. The centre also has its own baths. *Grænumörk 10 | heilsustofnun.is*

AROUND HVERAGERÐI

1 REYKJADALUR

Around 4km north of Hveragerði, 1 hr on foot

If you take the road leading north out of town, you'll reach the footpaths to Reykjadalur ("Steam Valley"). There is a car park and café next to the starting point, where you'll also come across Klambragilslaug, a geothermal pool in the warm river, where you can take a plunge. Be prepared to share it with crowds in summer, but in winter you stand a good chance of having it to yourself. It's important to wear sturdy shoes for walking in this area because of the extremely hot, often steaming, holes in the ground, which can even break through the soil! *F10*

INSIDER TIP
Take a dip

2 HELLISHEIÐI

18km west of Hveragerði, 20 mins by car

The *Hellisheiðarvirkjun* geothermal power plant is situated in the Hengill volcanic mountain range. Steam and hot water are pumped to the surface from a depth of over 2,000m. The steam is used to generate electricity and the hot water to heat the glacier water. This fresh water is then fed into Reykjavík's district-heating network.

Find out more about the technology, current projects and the region as a whole at the plant's visitor centre. There is also a café. *Daily 9am–5pm | admission including guided tour from 1,990 ISK (cheaper online), children up to 12 free | tel. 591 2880 | on.is/en/geothermalexhibition | F10*

SELFOSS

(▯ F10) **Selfoss (pop. 8,800) is the main trading centre of agricultural produce in the south. Admittedly, you may not fall in love with the town at first glance, but it is the perfect starting point for a trip. What's more, its infrastructure and location on the Ölfusá river provide it with a certain charm.**

Opened in 1929, a dairy that makes the traditional, nutritious, yoghurt-like *skyr* (see p. 29, Eating & Drinking) is still in operation. Legendary world chess champion Bobby Fischer lived out his last years here.

Strokkur geyser

EATING & DRINKING

FJÖRUBORÐIÐ

This rustic restaurant is famous for its king prawns. Reykjavík city-dwellers will travel to the country just for this … and the sensational sea view. *Daily noon–9pm | Eyrarbraut 3a | Stokkseyri | tel. 483 1550 | ££–£££*

KAFFI-KRÚS

Cosy, nostalgic, with fine pastries and cakes. *Daily 8.30am–8pm, Fri/Sat until 11pm | Austurvegur 7 | tel. 482 1266 | £*

SPORT & ACTIVITIES

KAJAKAFERÐIR

You can take a kayak tour along the coastline and on lakes and rivers in the surrounding area, depending on availability. A great choice for kids; pick-up available. *From 4,950 ISK, children (6–14) 1,350 ISK | Heiðarbrún 24 | Stokkseyri | tel. 695 2058 and 868 9046 | kajak.is*

AROUND SELFOSS

3 REYKHOLT

40km northeast of Selfoss, 35 mins by car

A hissing and steaming township where most of Iceland's vegetables are grown in greenhouses of all sizes using geothermal energy. In the huge, bright greenhouses at *Friðheimar (daily noon–4pm, booking essential | tel. 496 88 94 | fridheimar.is)*, staff sell the produce and offer delights made with the tomatoes they grow all year round – like the Healthy Mary, a drink made from green tomatoes and ginger. Their tomato soup is also Iceland's best. *(G9)*

INSIDER TIP
Healthy Mary not Bloody Mary

4 GEYSIR ★

65km northeast of Selfoss, 1 hr by car or a day trip from Reykjavík

Wait, what's all the fuss about? Sometimes you can't even see the *Strokkur* geyser because of the crowds ... until it shoots its jets of water into the air. It is reliably active, while the nearby *Geysir* is less so. Still, its 14m-diameter pool is surrounded by fascinating sinter deposits. There are many smaller springs, with deposits in shades from turquoise to red, depending on the minerals occurring. Your best bet is to visit the thermal area in winter or on a late summer evening. *(G9)*

INSIDER TIP
Avoid the crowds

5 GULLFOSS ★

72km northeast of Selfoss, 1 hr by car

One of Iceland's most stunning waterfalls lies just 7km from the Geysir: the Gullfoss ("Golden Waterfall"). The glacial Hvítá river plunges down in twin cascades, at a 90° angle to each other, into the *Hvítárgljúfur* gorge. The 31m-high waterfall and gorge are protected sites. There is an exhibition about Gullfoss at the upper car park, as well as a shop and a café. *(H9)*

HVOLSVÖLLUR

(G11) **While it might not be the country's number one tourist attraction, Hvolsvöllur is a great base for exploring the surrounding area. For example, you can follow in the footsteps of *Njál's Saga* from here.**

Hvolsvöllur has been a commercial centre for decades. The region's first cooperative society was founded here in the 1930s – the town was a convenient location for farms in the south.

SIGHTSEEING

SAGA CENTRE

Love vintage and retro? This is the museum for you. Yes, everything is a little dusty, but the content is excellent. *Njál's Saga* is one of the most famous Icelandic sagas and revolves around wise Njál and his friend Gunnar, who fall victim to the thirst for revenge of Gunnar's wife, Hallgerður. *Daily 4–10pm | admission free | Hlíðarvegur 14*

LAVA CENTRE

This interactive museum is an amazing hands-on learning experience and you can easily spend the whole day here. Learn everything there is to know about volcanoes, earthquakes and Iceland's birth story.

INSIDER TIP **Feel the earth move**

You actually feel an earthquake and can hear the lava erupting. The rooftop view of the peaceful and green surroundings is relaxing. *June–Aug 9am–6pm, Sept–May 9am–4pm | film and exhibition 3,990 ISK, children 12 and over 1,990 ISK, family ticket 9,975 ISK | Austurvegur 14 | tel. 415 5200 | lavacentre.is*

EATING & DRINKING

KATLA

The restaurant inside the *Lava Centre (see above)* mainly serves dishes incorporating regional ingredients, including vegetarian options. A favourite with the locals. *Daily 9am–9pm | ££*

AROUND HVOLS VÖLLUR

6 HLÍÐARENDI

15km east of Hvolsvöllur, 30 mins by car

INSIDER TIP **Legendary resting place**

A key stop as you follow in the footsteps of *Njál's Saga*. The farm and supposed burial mound of Njál's friend Gunnar lie in the picturesque *Fljótsdalur* valley, with its verdant slopes and many waterfalls. Instead of fleeing for his life, Gunnar, captivated by the beauty of his farm, remained in the country and was slain. From here, you have a fabulous view of the plain and river, encircled by green sloping hills. A little church completes this idyllic picture-postcard scene. *H11*

7 SELJALANDSFOSS

20km east of Hvolsvöllur, 30 mins by car

Car after car fills the car park: the 40m-high *Seljalandsfoss* is one of Iceland's most popular waterfalls. It belongs to a group of smaller cascades that crash down the vertical escarpments of the Eyjafjallajökull volcano. What's special about Seljalandsfoss is the fact you can walk behind the cascading stream of water. Remember your waterproofs! *H11*

8 ÞÓRSMÖRK ★

40km east of Hvolsvöllur, at the end of mountain road F 249, 1½ hrs by jeep, better by bus

"The forest of the God of Thunder" is a hiking paradise encircled by three protective glaciers. So lace up your hiking boots and set off on the trails through lush vegetation and over sublime hills. Rushing glacial rivers only add to the experience. At the weekend, the area is popular with young Icelanders who come to party, but you can still find quiet, cosy spots. There is a kiosk and a campsite. Starting in Þórsmörk, you can set off on a four-day trek to *Landmannalaugar (J10)* or hike in two days to *Skógar (J11)*. *Ferðafélags Íslands (Mörkinni 6, Reykjavík | tel. 568 2533 | fi.is)* and *Útivist (Laugavegur*

178 | Reykjavík | tel. 562 1000 | utivist.is) offer guided hikes and accommodation in mountain cabins. *J11*

9 HEKLA ★

50km northeast of Hvolsvöllur, 1½ hrs by car, buses to Landmannalaugar stop on request

The Hekla volcano has been smoking and spewing for thousands of years and is often marked with a flame on old maps of Iceland. The 4km-long fissure vent is visible from a distance and at 1,491m high, the colcano was considered the gateway to Hell until well into the 18th century. After all, this was the only way people could explain the devastating eruptions like the one in 1104, when a flourishing settlement in the Þjórsádalur valley was destroyed. Still, the many outbursts have turned the area around Hekla into an impressive lava-clad landscape. The easiest ascent is from the north and is rewarded by a stunning view across the Highlands. A four-wheel drive will take you almost to the top. The *Hekla Centre* is an excellent source of information on both the volcano and the surrounding area *(daily 10am–10pm | at Hótel Leirubakki on Rte. 26 | admission 1,000 ISK). H10*

HEIMAEY

(G12) **The Vestmannaeyjar Islands ("Westman Islands") lie to the southwest of Iceland. The southernmost of these, Surtsey, was only formed between 1963 and 1967.**

Follow the Laugavegur trail to the Hekla volcano

The largest island is ★ Heimaey, which has had two peaks since the legendary eruption of 1973. Today, the island feels like a different world. Its manageable size (its total area is just 11.3km²) makes it easy to explore on foot. On 23 January 1973 the island shot to fame when a volcano erupted. Lava shot out of a 1.6km-long crevasse, gushing out, smothering houses and threatening to close the entrance to the harbour. The eruption lasted five months, and the ash buried a third of all the island's buildings. Today, Heimaey is a green island again, and its resourceful residents see the lava as a welcome source of building material. The cooled lava at the entrance to the harbour provides good protection against the northeasterly wind.

From Eldfell and the old *Helgafell* volcano, you get a panoramic view of the entire island as far as the south coast of Iceland and the Eyjafjallajökull and Mýrdalsjökull glaciers. The *Herjólfur* ferry plies the route between Landeyjahöfn and Heimaey several times a day, in stormy weather travelling from Þorlákshöfn. *Return ticket: 4,000 ISK (from Landeyjahöfn and Þorlákshöfn) | tel. 481 2800 | herjolfur.is*

SIGHTSEEING

ELDHEIMAR

The "Fire World" museum, which opened in 2014, documents the volcanic eruptions on Heimaey and its effects, including the creation of Surtsey. You can hear first hand how loud an eruption really is. *10 May–15 Sept daily 11am–5pm, 16 Sept–9 May daily 1.30–4.30pm | admission 2,900 ISK | Gerðisbraut 10 | eldheimar.is*

Puffins on the Vestmannaeyjar islands

SKANSINS

The fortifications above the harbour were constructed by the Danes in the 16th century, but they could not repel the assault by North African pirates in 1627, who carried off half the population into slavery. Parts of their ship's gear can be seen in the Folk Museum. A replica wooden stave church, a present from Norway to the Icelanders in 2000 on the occasion of the 1,000th anniversary of Christianisation, stands alongside the site. Also close by is Landlyst, Iceland's first maternity hospital (1847), now a museum. *Museum 15 May–15 Sept daily 11am–5pm | admission 500 ISK*

KLETTSVÍK

INSIDER TIP **See whales up close**

Save the whales! A whale sanctuary was opened here in March 2019 and its first guests were two beluga whales. The motivation behind the centre is not just charitable – the aim is also to create jobs and attract tourists. You can only visit the bay by boat. Afterwards, visit the *Sealife Trust* exhibition and rescue centre – they have puffins too! *2 April–2 Oct Mon–Sat 10am–4pm, Sun 1–4pm | Ægisgata 2 | tel. 540 2700 | admission 3,050 ISK, boat trip and centre admission 9,900 ISK | sealifetrust.com*

STÓRHÖFÐI

A coastal hike along the western shores of the island to its most southerly peak, *Stórhöfði*, is an enjoyable and relaxing experience. On a clear day, it also offers amazing views of the uninhabited neighbouring islands. Thousands of seabirds can be spotted nesting in the cliffs. The large colonies of puffins are particularly worth seeing. Stórhöfði also has a weather station and a splendid view over to Surtsey.

SURTSEY

An undersea volcanic eruption formed the island over a period of four years. The process began on 14 November 1963, and the lava flow finally came to a halt on 5 June 1967. Since then, surf and climatic influences have permanently changed the face of the island, which is now a strictly protected area and was granted World Heritage Site status by UNESCO in 2008. For tourists, boat excursions or sightseeing flights are the only opportunity to take a look at Surtsey. Information: *Viking Tours (see Sport & activities).* G12

EATING & DRINKING

BROTHERS BREWERY

This local brewery won a national prize for its beer in 2016. You can sample all the varieties in its pub. *Sept–April Thu 4pm–midnight, Fri 4pm–1am, Sat 2pm–1am, May–Aug Wed/Thu 4pm–midnight, Fri 4pm–1am, Sat 2pm–1am | Bárustígur 7 | tbb.is*

GOTT

Popular among locals for its good food made with fresh ingredients, ranging from fish to vegetarian dishes. *Daily 11.30am–9.30pm, Fri/Sat until 10pm | Bárustigur 11 | tel. 481 3060 | £–££*

SLIPPURINN EATERY

This former machinery room at the shipyard has been turned into a cosy restaurant. The menu reflects tradition (they even serve grilled mink whale steak), combined with fresh herbs and new flavour ideas. *4 May–10 Sep Wed–Sun 5–11pm (kitchen open until 10pm) | Strandvegur 76 | tel. 481 1515 | slippurinn.com | ££–£££*

SPORT & ACTIVITIES

You can book excursions by boat around the island, including bird- and whale-watching trips, at *Viking Tours (Heiðarvegur 59 | tel. 488 4800 | vikingtours.is).*

Fancy a cliff-top group hike or a RIB boat excursion? Or would you prefer an individual guide? *Seabirds and Cliffs Adventures (Ægisgata 1 | tel. 893 2150 | saca.is)* is your port of call for all of these.

FESTIVALS

Heimaey celebrates some special festivals:

13th Day of Christmas: 6 January; the 13 Christmas elves and their troll parents parade through the town with torches; concludes with fireworks.

End of the volcanic eruption: first weekend of July; music and dancing to commemorate the end of the lava flow.

National holiday: first weekend in August; in 1874 when Iceland

Vík í Mýrdal: gigantic cliffs line the coast as far as Reynisdrangar

celebrated its first steps to full independence, island inhabitants were unable to attend in Þingvellir and instead celebrated on the island. The locals have kept up the tradition, with music and cliff climbing the order of the day. Book accommodation well in advance if you want to join in the celebrations.

BEACHES

There is a splendid beach along the west coast to Stórhöfði, which is a popular spot for (sun)bathing in summer.

VÍK Í MÝRDAL

(▥ J12) **Vík is the southernmost village in Iceland. It is situated at the foot of the Reynisfjall ridge (340m) amid green meadows and surrounded by black glacial outwash plains and pebble beaches.**

Birdwatchers will find thousands of seabirds here, including Arctic terns and the northern fulmar, which also nests here. Vík lies at the heart of the 9,500km² *Katla Geopark (katlageopark.is)* that stretches from Hvolsvöllur up to the Vatnajökull.

SIGHTSEEING

REYNISDRANGAR

Three rocky basalt stacks rise from the sea to the south of Reynisfjall, the highest of them measuring 66m. On your way there, you will pass a commemorative stone in memory of drowned sailors from German fishing boats. Legend has it that the Reynisdrangar are fossilised trolls.

EATING & DRINKING

SVARTA FJARAN

The "Black Beach" restaurant lies directly at the Dyrhólaós estuary. Alongside tastily prepared dishes, including vegetarian options, are homemade cakes. *Daily 11am–8pm | at the end of route 215 | tel. 571 2718 | svartafjaran.com | £*

BEACHES

DYRHÓLAÓS ☂

This black lava beach on the spit is one of the most beautiful in the country. White breakers crashing to the shore, lava pebbles and accessible caves framed by columns of basalt make for a dream in black and white.

AROUND VÍK Í MÝRDAL

10 DYRHÓLAEY

19km west of Vík, 20 mins by car

This promontory to the west of Vík rises 120m out of the sea and takes its name – "Door Hill Island" – from its natural rock archway jutting off the coast. A lighthouse, built in 1910, stands on the cape. From here, you have a breathtaking view of the sea and the glacier landscape. *J12*

11 SKÓGAR

33km west of Vík, 25 mins by car

You'd be hard-pushed to find someone who hasn't seen a picture of stunning waterfall *Skógafoss*, which thunders 60m down into the valley near the small village of Skógar. A journey to its top (by stairs and a pathway) reveals a dramatic view down into the huge volume of water from above. Be sure to continue along the path as you will soon find yourself alone and see countless other small waterfalls.

INSIDER TIP
Multiple waterfalls

When the sun shines, people say you can see the shimmering chest of gold hidden behind the waterfall by Skógar's first settler. When a boy once tried to fetch the chest, he only managed to grab the handle, which is now on show at the *Skógar Open-Air Museum (Daily June–Aug 9am–6pm, Sept/Oct, May 10am–5pm, Nov–April 10am–4pm | café: June–Aug daily 10am–5pm | admission 2,300 ISK | skogasafn.is)*. Among other things, the museum traces the history of island transport. *J11*

WHERE TO SLEEP IN THE SOUTH

DESIGN AT THE GEOTHERMAL POWER PLANT

This unusual hotel is located at the heart of the lava landscape near the Nesjavellir geothermal power station. The *ION Adventure Hotel* has won its fair share of awards for its low-rise design that blends seamlessly into the lava, but even more exciting is its commitment to sustainability, from the building materials used to the food served. The view from the hot pot and sauna is also a hit. If you're a bit of a tech geek, you can even see the power station. Luckily, the furnishing inside the rooms is a little more chic! *Nesjavellir við Þingvallavatn | ionadventure.ioniceland.is | £££*

THE EAST

THE ICE AGE AND GLACIERS

This region really has the wow factor – something it owes to the elemental forces of nature that have shaped it and are still at work to this day. This is a landscape under the spell of the Vatnajökull glacier: vast swathes of the land south of Iceland's largest glacier have been silted up by its countless outflows, while regular volcanic eruptions under the ice sheet still lead to glacial flows that have, over many centuries, transformed the once-green landscape into a beguiling wasteland.

In spring, the Vatnajökull glacier overlooks swathes of Alaskan lupin

Along the east coast, the deep fjords, formed by Ice Age glaciers, are framed by steep, towering ridges. These formations are composed of the oldest types of rock on the island. Basalt, easily recognisable by its column-like structure, dominates, but the somewhat surreal colour spectrum of the mountains – which changes according to climatic and light conditions – is down to the presence of rhyolite.

Once key trading and fishing centres, today, many of the small coastal villages and towns are fighting for survival.

THE EAST

NORÐURLAND
EYSTRA
AUSTURLAND
1
100km, 1¼ hrs
8 Kárahnjúkar Dam
75km, 1 hr
1
Höfn
p.72
1 Jökulsárlón
2 Skaftafell

MARCO POLO HIGHLIGHTS

★ **JÖKULSÁRLÓN**
Glide among the icebergs, with their white, blue and black tones, on a boat tour of the lake ➤ p. 72

★ **SKAFTAFELL**
At the foot of Iceland's largest glacier, Vatnajökull, in the centre of the national park of the same name, lies a green paradise with hiking trails, a hot spring and glacier tongues ➤ p. 73

★ **HALLORMSSTAÐUR**
Iceland's only "real" forest lies beside Lake Lagarfljót ➤ p. 76

HÖFN

(▯ Q9) **This village, whose name simply means "harbour", is the administrative and commercial centre for the southeast. The place celebrated its heyday in the 19th century, while today its charm lies in its picturesque setting at the foot of the Vatnajökull ice cap.**

Close to the harbour, you'll find the *recreation area* and the *Ósland Bird Sanctuary*, home to the great northern diver, Arctic tern and whooper swan.

SIGHTSEEING

GAMLABÚÐ

This museum featuring local history, the geology of the Vatnajökull and nature lies in the old town centre at the harbour and is home to several small exhibitions. In two other buildings, boats and other artifacts tell about the lives of fishermen in the 19th century. *Daily June–Aug 9am–6pm, May/Sept until 5pm | admission free | Heppuvegur 1 | vatnajokulsthjodgardur.is*

EATING & DRINKING

KAFFI HORNIÐ

A local institution that's always experimenting with something new. King prawns are a must here, but the menu also offers vegan options. *Daily from 11.30am | Hafnarbraut 42 | tel. 478 2600 | kaffihornid.is | ££*

SPORT & ACTIVITIES

GLACIER JEEPS

Drive over Iceland's largest glacier, first by four-wheel-drive and then, for the last leg of the journey, head up the Vatnajökull by snowmobile. Various tours are available all year round. *3-hr excursion with 1 hr by snowmobile 22,000 ISK/pers | off the Ring Road, junction F 985 | tel. 478 1000 | glacierjeeps.is*

HÖFN LOCAL GUIDE

INSIDER TIP **Dine with locals**

Exploring Höfn with Hulda is a real treat because you get to dine with the locals. She also knows a huge amount about the place and offers walks with yoga. *Hafnarbraut 41 | tel. 864 4952 | hofnlocalguide.com*

AROUND HÖFN

1 JÖKULSÁRLÓN ★

75km southwest of Höfn, 45 mins by car, 1 hr by bus

Fun fact: some scenes from *Game of Thrones* were filmed here. The *Breiðamerkurjökull* glacier runs into this 200m-deep lake; the scene is one of countless icebergs drifting across the backdrop of Vatnajökull. Enjoy some fascinating perspectives on a trip on the lake with *Glacier Lagoon (6,000 ISK, children 6–12 3,000 ISK | tel. 478 2122 | icelagoon.is),* either by amphibious boat or Zodiac; in high season you should book ahead. You can feel the cold of the ice and even touch it! After your trip, you can recharge your batteries at the *restaurant (daily June–Sept 9am–7pm, March–May, Oct 9am–6pm, Nov–Feb 9am–5pm | tel. 478 2122 | £)* with its fine view across the lagoon. *O10*

2 SKAFTAFELL ★

135km west of Höfn, around 1½ hrs by car

Right in the middle of the Vatnajökull National Park – at 13,600 km² the largest in Europe – is the green idyll of Skaftafell nature reserve, which extends between the icy tongues of the Morsárjökull and Skaftafellsjökull glaciers. Over 210 plant species grow here, and bird life is plentiful and varied too. There are many hiking trails criss-crossing the reserve. Popular spots with visitors are the *Svartifoss* waterfall and the *Sjónarsker* observation point, facing out over the glacier and the desert-like plain, the Skeiðarársandur. You can also take part in a guided hike up Iceland's highest mountain, *Hvannadalshnúkur* (2,119m). Find information at the *Service Centre (tel. 478 300 | vjp.is)* in the park. *N10*

Svartifoss waterfall

DJÚPIVOGUR

(R7) **This little village is known for its granite egg sculptures.**

The 34 sculptures in the shape of birds' eggs created by Sigurður Guðmundsson are an attractive addition to the village. Lining the coastal road in Gleðivík Bay, the coloured, polished natural stones resemble the real things, laid by species native to Djúpivogur – they're just a lot bigger! Otherwise, there's not much else going on in the 400-year-old trading post, whose inhabitants make a living from fishing or tourism.

SIGHTSEEING

The Búlandnes promontory on which the village is located is peppered with lakes and is a designated birdwatching site; a number of signs have been erected to this effect. The beautiful circular trail starts above the school: to the sound of birdsong and amid swathes of flowers, you will discover the vast landscape and magnificent views over the sea. A total of 26 bird species nest and live here around the waters – from mallard and whooper swans to long-necked guillemots and beautifully patterned harlequin ducks. Just make sure to remember your binoculars!

EATING & DRINKING

LANGABUÐ

The oldest house here has grown into the heart of the village, with bingo, music, exhibitions and a café. It's hugely popular with visitors in summer, but that is probably no surprise given the quality of the cakes! Also serves small plates. *Daily 10am–5pm | tel. 478 8820 | £*

INSIDER TIP
Delicious cakes

AROUND DJÚPIVOGUR

3 PAPEY

15km southeast of Djúpivogur

Until the year CE 900, Irish monks lived on the largest of the islands off Djúpivogur; you can still see ruins from the period and an abandoned farm. Papey is an ideal destination for birdwatching. *Enquire about boat times ahead of travel | djupivogur.is/Djupivogur/Nattura/Papey |* *R8*

4 TEIGARHORN

4km from Djúpivogur, 45 mins on foot, 15 mins by car

A nature reserve named after Teigarhorn Farm at the foot of the pyramid-shaped, basalt *Búlandstindur*

The large stone eggs at Djúpivogur are modelled on those of endemic bird species

mountain (1,069m). The spot is well known as a source of beautiful stones and renowned as an excavation site for zeolite crystals.

INSIDER TIP
Crystals everywhere

Even more fascinating are the scolecites, needle-shaped crystals formed in clusters, good examples of which are on display in the *museum (June–Aug 9am–4pm | tel. 869 6550 | teigarhorn.is)*; go and take a look for yourself! *R7*

EGILSSTAÐIR

(R5) **This relatively new town (founded in 1944) is now the centre of the eastern region.**

The national forestry office of Iceland is based here, and it is also home to a jazz club and the *Sláturhús* cultural centre *(slaturhusid.is)*. Egilsstaðir is a good place to start for trips into the eastern Highlands and the small coastal villages, as well as to Lagarfljót lake (also known as Lögurinn) and Hallormsstaður forest.

SIGHTSEEING

MINJASAFN AUSTURLANDS

The *East Iceland Heritage Museum* documents life in the region from the time of settlement up to the 19th century. Two permanent exhibitions deal with life in the country and reindeer, which only live in the east of Iceland. *Daily June–Aug 10am–6pm, Sept–May Tue–Fri 11am–4pm | admission 1,200 ISK | Laufskógar 1 | minjasafn.is*

EATING & DRINKING

KAFFI NIELSEN

Located in a pretty, old house, this cosy restaurant is busy all day long. The leafy outdoor terrace is popular on sunny days. The new Icelandic-inspired dishes are made from regional ingredients and are truly excellent. *7 June–31 Aug Tue–Sat 11.30am–9pm | Tjarnarbraut 1 | tel. 471 2001 | ££–£££*

SPORT & ACTIVITIES

How about taking the 68km bike tour around Lagarfljót lake – perhaps as training for the annual tour in August? *Bike hire: Egilsstaðastofa, Kaupvangur 17 at the campsite | 3,000 ISK per day*

WELLNESS

VÖK BATH

Relax in four pools set into Urriðavatn lake. The water comes (naturally) from warm springs to create the ultimate bathing experience. There is also a bistro here. *June–Aug 11am–11pm | admission from 5,990 ISK | Egilsstaðir | tel. 470 9500 | vokbaths.is*

AROUND EGILSSTAÐIR

5 LAGARFLJÓT

68km round trip by bike

Some 3km wide and 30km long, the lake is fed by a number of glacial rivers and narrows to form the Lagarfljót river. Legend has it that a giant worm-like monster, Ormur, lives on the bed of the lake! At the *Atlavík campsite (1500 ISK/tent | tel. 470 2070)*, you can sleep under the trees and lose yourself on walks in the forest – perfect for the romantic at heart. Q–R 4–6

6 HALLORMSSTAÐUR ★

12km south of Egilsstaðir, 20 mins by car

Yes, there is a real forest in Iceland! In fact, many of its trees are over 100 years old. Thanks to the favourable soil conditions and the almost continental climate, the coniferous and deciduous trees enjoy ideal growing conditions. Information boards guide you through the natural beauty of your surroundings. Q6

7 SKRIÐUKLAUSTUR

45km southwest of Egilsstaðir, 1 hr by car

In 1939, author Gunnar Gunnarsson built this strikingly different 1,000m² house to plans by German architect Fritz Höger. But back in the 16th century, a monastery stood on the site on the southwest bank of the Lagarfljót. Today the house hosts a cultural centre which, among other things, stages exhibitions about Gunnarsson and has a great café. The homemade jams are a real hit, especially the rhubarb and angelica flavours. Head outside to see the excavations of the monastery. *June–Aug daily 10am–6pm (café open same hours) | admission 1,100 ISK | tel. 471 2990 | skriduklaustur.is* | Q6

INSIDER TIP Delicious jams!

8 KÁRAHNJÚKAR DAM

100km from Egilsstaðir, around 1¼ hrs by car

The new, well-developed 910 road leads to an information platform from where you can see the dam and the 57km² *Hálslón reservoir*. Around two thirds of the way to the dam, you will come across a hot put with a cabin. You can head out on hikes from here – it's a real oasis. *laugarfell.is* | O7

9 SEYÐISFJÖRÐUR

27km east of Egilsstaðir, 30 mins by car

If you arrive by ferry, the picturesque village is your first point of contact with Iceland. In the 19th century, it used to be the country's largest commercial settlement; the well-preserved wooden houses date back to this period. Alongside its rich cultural programme of museums and summer concerts, Seyðisfjörður is a good starting point for hikes in the eastern fjord region. In winter, however, the fjord and mountains can start to feel a little oppressive. Remember the 2017 mini-series *Trapped*? The harbour scenes were filmed here. German artist Lukas Kühne has created a "walk-in" sound sculpture, comprised of five linked concrete domes (2–5m in diameter and 2–4m high) each with a different resonance. The acoustics inside *Tvísöngur* are excellent and best tried out by singing! *visit seydisfjordur.com/tvisongur* | R5

INSIDER TIP Sing a sweet song

10 BAKKAGERÐI

65km north of Egilsstaðir, 1 hr by car (mountain roads/gravel tracks)

Picturesque Seyðisfjörður is a study in blue and green

Bakkagerði is a tiny, hidden hamlet surrounded by a mountainous landscape, framed by a backdrop of rugged and colourful rhyolite and basalt peaks. The seemingly enchanted village stands at the foot of the small Álfaborg hill, where the elf queen supposedly lives, a must-see for elf lovers. The place is also popular with ornithologists who come here for up-close viewing of the nesting puffins – great fun, especially when you can get so close to them on the cliffs. They are within touching distance, but get too close and they will disappear inside their nesting caves. The best time for puffin-watching is from the start of June to mid-August. *(▯ S4)*

INSIDER TIP
See the puffins

THE NORTHEAST

130km from Egilsstaðir to Vopnafjördur, 3 hrs by car (some roads are gravel)

Venture off the tourist path to the far northeast of Iceland, with the Melrakkaslétta plain and small coastal villages like *Raufarhöfn (▯ O1)* and *Vopnafjörður (▯ Q4)*. While these were once thriving fishing villages, today they are struggling to scrape by. You won't encounter many other visitors here and will often be treated to the views of the coastal landscape with no one else in sight. Still, there is plenty of accommodation and a wide range of things to do in the area.

The mysterious stone arches of *Arctic Henge* in Raufarhöfn are an unforgettable sight. And just 15km from Vopnafjörður in Selárdalur is a small *thermal swimming pool (daily 7am–11pm | free entry | tel. 473 1499)*. illuminated by candles, the moon and, sometimes, the ethereal beauty of the northern lights. A romantic's dream!

THE NORTH

ANCIENT HEROES AND FAST HORSES

Do you love the outdoors? Hiking, horse-riding, skiing, mountain biking or rafting? Rugged coastlines, steep peaks and vast lava landscapes? Ancient sagas and history? Seals, whales and plenty of ducks? Then the north is the region for you.

The north is a chequered landscape stretching from the northwest fjords to the Highlands. One of the most impressive areas in terms of geology and scenery is the Mývatn region, which is chock-full of natural monuments.

Explore the stunning Mývatn region by mountain bike

The main centre of population is Akureyri, a mini-metropolis with art, culture and ski slopes galore. The many historic sites dotted around the Skagafjörður area, once home to key trading centres and Iceland's second bishopric, are worth a look. Skagafjörður is also famous for horse-breeding.

THE NORTH

MARCO POLO HIGHLIGHTS

★ **MÝVATN**
It's not only ducks that love this lake with its tree-lined banks ➤ p. 82

★ **DETTIFOSS**
Miniature version of the Niagara Falls and Iceland's largest waterfall ➤ p. 83

★ **JÖKULSÁRGLJÚFUR NATIONAL PARK**
Iceland's largest waterfall is a miniature version of the Niagara Falls ➤ p. 83

★ **HÓLAR**
Iceland's historic second bishopric, with the oldest stone church in the country ➤ p. 88

MÝVATNS SVEIT

(📖 M–N 4) **A place to experience the dreamlike landscapes created by the power of volcanoes. It's not surprising that several scenes from *Game of Thrones* were filmed around the "Mosquito Lake".**

The area lies on a plain 230m above sea level and is right in the heart of the rift zone, the rift valley system between the North American and Eurasian continental plates. It never stops hissing and bubbling here, thanks to the many hot springs and volcanoes.

SIGHTSEEING

NÁMASKARÐ

An expanse of solfataras (natural volcanic steam vents) cloaks the base of Námafjall (482m), each belching out sulphur from the springs below that shimmer in a variety of colours. The temperature of the mud pots can reach 100°C, and the lighter-coloured parts of the surface crust, in particular, can cave in easily. Sulphur was extracted here for hundreds of years for use in the manufacture of gunpowder. *📖 N4*

Solfataras surround Námaskarð

DIMMUBORGIR

The lava formations at Dimmuborgir have a fabulous, otherworldly character. Here, you'll come across tunnels and caves with names like *kirkjan*, "the Church". The "Dark Castles", the literal translation of Dimmuborgir, lie in a mysterious, enchanted hollow where the bizarre lava formations are piled up, sometimes wholly overgrown by birch trees and creepers. These unique lava sculptures were created around 2,000 years ago when molten lava flowed out of the lava lake that was once here. *📖 N4*

HVERFELL

From Dimmuborgir, a signposted path on the north side leads first through lava and then over Hverfellssandur to the striking Hverfell crater. With an incredible kilometre-wide diameter and a depth of 140m, it is both one of the largest and most beautiful explosion craters in the world. The entire area is a protected nature reserve. *📖 N4*

MÝVATN ★

Iceland's fourth-biggest lake is characterised by fascinating lava formations and rich vegetation along its banks. Calling all birdwatchers: this is the place for you. As well as other birds, over 15 species of duck breed here in large colonies, drawn by the favourable climate and plentiful supply of mosquitos (in larvae form), from which the lake takes its name. The grown mosquitos are annoying, but they don't actually bite. Numerous springs issue from the bottom of the lake, which has a maximum depth of 5m.

The fine *Fuglasafn Sigurgeirs (Bird Museum, daily June–Aug noon–5pm, Sept–May 2–4pm | admission 2,200 ISK | fuglasafn.is)*, featuring stuffed specimens of regional birdlife, stands on the northwest bank. The atmosphere in this thoroughly modern showcase, though, is anything but stuffy! A café overlooks the lake. *M–N4*

EATING & DRINKING

GAMLI BÆRINN

The old farmhouse is now a cosy café, serving cakes and light bites made from regional produce such as trout. *Daily 11.30am–11pm | Reykjahlíð | tel. 464 4270 | f | N4*

SPORT & ACTIVITIES

THE NORTHERN LIGHTS

Nestled in snow, Mývatn's landscape is transformed into a fairytale world, making it well worth a winter trip. The Northern Lights are particularly beautiful here. *Geo Travel (geotravel.is)* offers a wide range of winter activities, from dog sledding to ski tours.

WELLNESS

MÝVANT NATURE BATHS

Bathing in turquoise blue, mineral waters surrounded by a lava landscape is a dream and there is no nicer place on Mývatn lake than this lagoon with natural baths. *Daily June–21 Aug 10am–11pm, 22 Aug–May noon–10pm | 5,900 ISK, book ahead | tel. 464 4411 | myvatnnaturebaths.is*

AROUND MÝVATNSSVEIT

1 DETTIFOSS ★

Around 40km northeast of Mývatnssveit, 40 mins by car

A waterfall with wow factor: plunging 44m into the deep, Mother Nature has crafted a little brother for the Niagara Falls here, a gigantic, 100m-wide cascade. The sheer mass of water from the glacial river Jökulsá á Fjöllum envelops the surrounding area in a cloud of spray lit up by dazzling rainbows. *N–O4*

2 JÖKULSÁRGLJÚFUR NATIONAL PARK ★

40km northeast of Mývatnssveit, 45 mins by car

The national park stretches from Dettifoss for over 30km as far as Route 85 to the north and is today part of the large Vatnajökull National Park. The 25km-long and up to 120m-deep

Jökulsárgljúfur canyon, into which several waterfalls spill their load, is breathtaking. A hiking trail leads along the gorge to the *Vesturdalur* valley some 16km away. Close by, you'll find the *Hlóðaklettar* basalt formations, nicknamed the "Echoing Rocks". From *Vesturdalur*, a further day's hike takes you through lush vegetation to *Ásbyrgi (🕮 N3)*, a horseshoe-shaped, thickly wooded ravine with steep sides stretching up almost 100m. *Visitor Centre Glúfrastofa: Ásbyrgi, at the campsite | tel. 470 7100 | vjp.is | 🕮 N3–4*

3 HÚSAVÍK

57km north of Mývatnssveit, 50 mins by car

The main attraction in this prettily situated fishing village are the *whale-watching tours (North Sailing | tel. 464 7272 | northsailing.is)* in restored oak boats. The *exhibition* provides in-depth information about all species of whales that live off Iceland's shores and whaling. The museum also houses a life-size whale skeleton. *June–Aug daily 9am–6pm, April/May, Sept/Oct daily 10am–5pm, Nov–March Tue–Sat 11am–4pm | admission 2,200 ISK, children free | Hafnarstétt 1 | tel. 414 2800 | whalemuseum.is | 🕮 M3*

AKUREYRI

(🕮 L4) **Akureyri, or the "Pearl of the North" as the locals fondly call it, lies in an attractive spot in the Eyjafjörður region at the foot of Súlur (1,144m).**

VISITING AKUREYRI'S MUSEUMS

If you're planning on visiting several museums in Akureyri in one day, make sure to buy a day ticket (2,000 ISK), which grants entry to five different museums: Davíðshús, Akureyri Museum, Nonnahús, Akureyri Toy Museum and Laufás heritage site and musuem. You can buy your ticket at Akureyri Museum.

The town owes much of its charm to its many old villas and the profusion of trees, and manages to be both tranquil and urban at the same time. A university town and commercial centre, it is also an art hub, with plenty of museums and galleries. The best way to experience it is on a quiet stroll, especially through the old section, with its well-preserved houses.

SIGHTSEEING

HOF CULTURAL AND CONFERENCE CENTRE

Not only an architectural attraction, the cultural centre also serves as the *tourist information centre (Mon–Fri 8am–4pm)*. The round building, with its spacious interiors clad in dark grey basalt slabs, is the setting for regular exhibitions as well as a varied programme of music and theatre. There's also a good *restaurant (££)* with a terrace directly on the waterfront. Alongside salads, pasta and fish dishes, they also serve cakes. *Strandgata 12 | tel. 450 1000 | menningarhus.is*

LISTASAFN IN THE LISTAGIL

Three museums were merged together to create the Centre of Visual Arts in 2012: the Akureyri Art Museum (no. 12), the Ketilhús and the Deiglan. Following its refurbishment in 2017/18, the art museum offers even more space for exhibitions of contemporary Icelandic and international artists. Deiglan is only open for special events. *Daily noon–5pm | admission 1,900 ISK | Kaupvangsstræti 10 | listak.is*

AKUREYRARKIRKJA

Architect Guðjón Samúelsson looked to Iceland's basalt columns for inspiration for this striking church. Seventeen windows illustrate events from the history of Icelandic Christianity. One window in particular stands out; it was originally part of Coventry Cathedral in England and is 400 years old. *2 June–28 Aug daily 10am–4pm | concerts on Sundays in July*

BOTANICAL GARDEN

The botanical garden and city park is a green highlight. It contains both Iceland's native plants (approximately 430 species) as well as many plants from the Arctic region. Benches and a café practically beg you to stop and take a break. Founded in 1912 by Margrethe Schiöth, the garden is full of ancient trees and is one of the most beautiful in Iceland. *June–Sept Mon–Fri 8am–10pm, Sat/Sun 9am–10pm | free admission | Eyrarlandsvegur | lystigardur.akureyri.is*

DAVÍÐSHÚS

Head to the home of writer Davíð Stefánsson (1895–1964) to find out what life was like in one of the town's typical villas back in the 1950s. The rooms look as if he has just left and the library is one of the most valuable private book collections in Iceland. *June–Aug Mon–Fri 1pm–5pm | admission 900 ISK | Bjarkarstígur 6*

EATING & DRINKING

BAUTINN

A good restaurant with a nostalgic feel and a wide range of dishes, which has

Take a boat from Húsavík for a chance to see several species of whale

Water thunders over the horseshoe-shaped precipice at Goðafoss

attained something close to cult status. Whale and horsemeat are specialities and there's a reasonably priced salad bar, too. *Daily 11am–10pm | Hafnarstræti 92 | tel. 462 1818 | £–££*

BLÁA KANNAN

Cosy, popular café in the main shopping street that stands out because of its colour. A perfect stopping point for small plates and cakes. *Summer daily 8.30am–11.30pm, winter Mon–Fri 9am–11pm, Sat/Sun 10am–11.30pm | Hafnarstræti 96 | tel. 461 4600 | £*

SPORT & ACTIVITIES

Skjaldarvík Guesthouse (around 5km north of Akureyri on the 816 | tel. 552 5200 | skjaldarvik.is) offers horse-riding lessons *(11,900 ISK for 1 hr).* If you need sustenance too, you can add dinner for 15,900 ISK. Lessons especially for kids are also offered *(5,000 ISK).*

Ferðafélag Akureyrar (Strandgata 23 | tel. 462 2720 | ffa.is) offers guided hikes. Iceland's largest ski resort is *Hlíðarfjall (1-day lift pass 5,800 ISK, 1-day ski hire 5,900 ISK, incl. helmet and poles)*; in summer, the chairlift runs Fri–Sun and you can take a bike up before hurtling down the slope. *Tel. 462 2280 | hlidarfjall.is*

WELLNESS

AKUREYRI OUTDOOR SWIMMING POOL

Three water slides, a large hot tub with massage jets, a steam bath, sauna and even a place for sunbathing. This pool offers all the standard amenities with its 25m pool, as well as hot pots of varying temperatures. It's hard to imagine a more fun swimming pool! *All year Mon–Fri 6.45am–9pm, summer Sat/Sun 8am–7.30pm, winter Sat/Sun 9am–7pm | 1,100 ISK, 270 ISK children 6–17 | Þingvallastræti 21 | tel. 461 4455 | sundlaugar.is*

ÁRSKÓGSSANDI MICROBREWERY

Bjórböðin ("the Beer Bath") may remind you of times gone by when rulers would bathe in milk and honey. Well, here it's beer! You may not believe it but a 25-minute soak in warm beer followed by a chill-out session is the ultimate in relaxation, whether on your own or in a group. *Beer bath for 2 people 19,900 ISK | Ægisgata 31, 33km north of Akureyri | tel. 414 2828 | bjorbodin.is*

INSIDER TIP **Bathe in beer**

NIGHTLIFE

GRÆNI HATTURINN

Live Icelandic music several times a month. The best place in the north to meet great people: it's fun, loud and eventful! *Open during events (see website) | Hafnarstræti 96 | tel. 461 4646 | graenihatturinn.is*

AROUND AKUREYRI

4 GOÐAFOSS

35km east of Akureyri, 30 mins by car

The thundering Goðafoss waterfall cascades over a broad precipice with wide, horseshoe-shaped channels. It acquired its name, "Waterfall of the Gods", in the year 1000, when statues of the heathen gods were flung into the waters following the adoption of Christianity. *M4*

5 HRÍSEY

35km north of Akureyri, 30 mins by car plus 15 mins by ferry

At the heart of Eyjafjörður is this small island, without cars but with beautiful paths and diverse bird life. Lose yourself in this paradise of hills and cliffs. *Daily ferry from Árskógssandur | return ticket 1,700 ISK | hrisey.is | K3*

INSIDER TIP **Peaceful island paradise**

6 GRÍMSEY

41km north of the mainland

It's a 20-minute flight to Iceland's northernmost point: the remote island of Grímsey lies on the Arctic Circle (66° 30′ North). On request, every visitor can receive a certificate to document their visit. Beautiful hiking trails lead all over the island, where the towering 100m-high cliffs are a paradise for bird-watchers and home to some 30 species of seabirds. *Norlandair | 22,500 ISK | tel. 414 6960 | norlandair.is*

From Dalvík, there is a cheaper alternative by boat; journey time is three hours: *Sun/Mon, Wed–Fri | return ticket 8,000 ISK | tel. 458 8970 | saefari.is | L1*

SAUÐÁRKRÓKUR

(H4) **The statue at the entrance to the town shows that you are now entering horse territory. The old town still features many beautiful houses along the Aðalgata.**

Sauðárkrókur is located on the peninsula of Skagi, a good starting point for splendid hikes on the Tindastóll. Part of the classic *Grettir's Saga* is set on the nearby island of Drangey, and you can find out more about the outlaw's colourful life there.

EATING & DRINKING

HARD WOK CAFÉ

The furnishings alone warrant a visit to this establishment. Wok dishes are the mainstay but sandwiches and soups are also available. *June–Aug daily 11.30am–9.30pm | Aðalgata 8 | £–££*

AROUND SAUÐÁRKRÓKUR

7 DRANGEY

16km north of Sauðárkrókur, 20 mins by car

The steep cliffs of the island of Drangey tower some 200m out of the middle of the Skagafjörður fjord. Grettir, hero of his eponymous saga, spent the last three years of his life here, and he is even said to have swum to the island from his farm at Reykir. Many species of bird, including guillemots, build their nests here. Today, numbers at the seabird colonies have recovered, but in times of famine – especially in the 18th and 19th centuries – people used to hunt the birds and plunder their nests. It is said that 200,000 birds were slaughtered during a single spring. You'll find information on crossings at the restaurant or the Reykir campsite *(departures June–Aug daily 10am | 14,900 ISK | tel. 821 0090 | drangey.net)*. In Reykir, you can bathe in the hot *Grettislaug* springs *(admission 1,000 ISK | changing rooms available)*.

8 GLAUMBÆR

15km south of Sauðárkrókur, 20 mins by car

This picturesque 18th-century turf farm has been turned into a museum and is much-photographed! The site provides a snapshot of life on farms in rural Iceland until the early 20th century. Would you live here? *20 May–20 Sept daily 10am–6pm | admission 1,700 ISK | glaumbaer.is |* *J4*

9 HÓLAR ★

18km south of Sauðárkrókur, 20 mins by car

The former bishopric of Hólar lies at the heart of the scenic Hjaltadalur valley. Steeped in history, the diocese was founded in 1106 and has a number of interesting sites, including one of the oldest stone churches in the country. Hólar has been an educational centre for centuries and was also the site of the first printing press in the country (1530).

Today, the place is home to a college specialising in equine science and tourism, aquaculture and fish biology. The old schoolhouse hosts an exhibition tracing the history of the Icelandic horse, while an adjacent building houses a freshwater aquarium. *Centre of the Icelandic Horse: June–Aug Tue–Sun 10am–6pm |*

Glaumbær: see how Icelanders lived in decades gone by

admission 1,000 ISK. Cathedral church and Nýibær turf house: summer daily 10am–6pm, guided tours available | free admission | *J4*

10 HOFSÓS

33km northeast of Sauðárkrókur, 30 mins by car

It's hard to believe that this sleepy backwater town was once a hive of activity in the 19th century, when thousands of Icelanders waited here in anticipation of their voyage to the New World. In those days, Hofsós was an important trading centre with what was a large harbour for the period. Some of the emigrants managed to fulfill their dreams in the US and Canada but many returned disappointed. The *Icelandic Emigration Centre* tells the story of their fates and the new lives of the emigrants *(June–Aug daily 11am–6pm | admission 1,500 ISK | hofsos.is)*. Another Hofsós attraction is its spectacular fjord-front *swimming pool (daily 10pm–midnight | 4,900 ISK, by appointment only | tel. 867 2216)*.

In the evening music adds to the atmosphere as visitors swim under the evening sun in summer or the Northern Lights in winter in an infinity pool whose blue waters seem to blend seamlessly with the fjord. *J3*

INSIDER TIP
Infinite relaxation

WHERE TO SLEEP IN THE NORTH

UNUSUAL ART

Stairs lead down from the *Safnasafnið Apartment* straight into the Museum for Folklore and Outsider Art, a collection of works outside the cultural mainstream. The small flat itself is home to its fair share of small, fine pieces, too. The view looks out towards Akureryri, but who needs the town when there's so much to discover here? *Mid-May–late Aug | min. 2-night stay | Svalbarðströnd | tel. 461 4066 | safnasafnid.is/ibud | £££*

THE WEST

SAGAS, BEACHES AND SEAFARERS

Three regions that could hardly be more fascinating make up the west of Iceland. Firstly, there's the area between Borgarnes and Langjökull – with farmland, hot springs and many locations related to saga hero Egil Skallagrímsson.

Further north, the Snæfellsnes peninsula has the mysterious Snæfellsjökull glacier at its western tip. Today, the north coast has just a few larger fishing villages, of which Stykkishólmur is the most

You'll need a head for heights to enjoy the coastline at Steilküste Látrabjarg

important, although in centuries past there were many harbours and villages here. In the far northwest, the saw-toothed coast of the Westfjords is an unparalleled landscape of stark beauty and utter seclusion – a paradise for adventurers and hikers. Though local infrastructure is improving, residents are moving away from this remote paradise where nature still rules.

THE WEST

MARCO POLO HIGHLIGHTS

★ **DYNJANDI**
Iceland's most beautiful waterfall is close to the coast ➤ p. 94

★ **LÁTRABJARG**
The country's westernmost cliffs are home to thousands of seabirds ➤ p. 95

★ **SNÆFELLSJÖKULL NATIONAL PARK**
The famous glacier with a near-magical aura ➤ p. 97

Grænlandshaf
4 Hornstrandir
Húnaflói
VESTFIRÐIR
61
Blönduós
Hrútafjörður
1
68
60
NORÐURLAND
VESTRA
7 Eiríksstaðir
85km, 1½ hrs
1
VESTURLAND
Hraunfossar 10
11 Húsafell
Deildartunguhver 9
Borg á Mýrum 8
37km, 45 mins
Borgarnes
p.98
20 km
12.43 mi

ÍSAFJÖRÐUR

(📖 C3) **Even the first settler, Helgi Hrólfsson, was lured by Ísafjörður's location: sheltered and with more fish than you could wish for. To this day, the fishing industry is a main source of income for the inhabitants of the largest town in the Westfjords region. Head for the old part of town to find whole streets of cosy little houses.**

A *seamen's monument* at the cemetery pays tribute to the seafarers who drowned off the coast. A further hint at the close links to the sea is the *whalebone arch* in the park. Ísafjörður is the perfect starting point for travellers to the Westfjords.

SIGHTSEEING

BYGGÐASAFN VESTFJARÐA – WESTFJORDS FOLK MUSEUM

The museum is housed in a former warehouse dating back to the 18th century and documents not only maritime but also municipal history. It takes you back to a time when everything was simple and without luxury. You'll also come across endless versions of the most essential instrument to accompany sea shanties: the accordion. A thoroughly Icelandic, and very special, private collection. *June–Aug daily 9am–5pm | admission 1,300 ISK | Neðstakaupstaður | nedsti.is*

INSIDER TIP
Accordians galore

EATING & DRINKING

TJÖRUHÚSIÐ

Fish at its very best: the restaurant in the grounds of the museum is known for its fish buffet. You sit on benches at long tables squeezed into the old "tar house", as the restaurant's name translates. Book a table in advance in the evenings. *Daily noon–2pm, 7–10pm | Neðstikaupstaður | tel. 456 4419 | £–££*

SPORT & ACTIVITIES

VESTURFERÐIR/WEST TOURS

Everything fun in the area can be organised for you, including regional excursions, kayak tours, hikes and riding tours. *Aðalstræti 7 | tel. 456 5111 | westtours.is*

AROUND ÍSAFJÖRÐUR

1 DYNJANDI ★ ⚑

80km south of Ísafjörður, 1¼ hrs by car, incl. mountain and gravel roads

Water plunges into the depths below down a total of six steps at this dramatic waterfall. The white veil of water from the powerful cascade is an impressive 30m wide at the top and 60m at the bottom. Rather appropriately, the name means "the thundering one" and it is surely the country's most beautiful waterfall – just ask any Icelander! It is part of a protected nature reserve. *📖 C4*

2 SKRÍMLISETUR IN BÍLDUDALUR

120km south of Ísafjörður, 2 hrs by car, incl. mountain and gravel roads

Elves aren't the only magical creature Iceland has to offer: there are sea monsters too! Some even report sightings! The museum explores the secrets of the Icelandic monster in two darkened and eerily decorated rooms. Eye witnesses report their sightings on film. When you've found out all about the monsters, take a relaxing break in the café. There are also handicrafts and delicacies from the region, including from the salt works near Reykjanes.

INSIDER TIP **Local food and crafts**

Mid-May–mid-Sept daily 10am–6pm | admission 1,000 ISK | Strandgata 7 | tel. 456 6666 | skrimsli.is | B4

3 LÁTRABJARG ★

210km southwest of Ísafjörður, 3½ hrs by car

The *Bjargtangar* lighthouse marks the westernmost point in Iceland, and therefore Europe. It stands atop the cliffs of the 14km-long Látrabjarg peninsula, which, at their highest point, tower more than 440m above the sea. Thousands of seabirds nest here; alongside puffins, there is a huge colony of razorbills. A footpath takes you to the picturesque *Rauðisandur beach*, with its yellowy-red seashell sand. A4

4 HORNSTRANDIR

Day or boat trip only from Ísafjörður

With dramatic scenery, steep cliffs home to nesting birds and endless

Dynjandi is arguably Iceland's most beautiful waterfall

The modern church at Stykkishólmur

small fjords, the 580km² area in the far north is a hiker's paradise. Countless abandoned farmhouses and the rich vegetation that has flourished in the absence of sheep create a real atmosphere. Foxes roam everywhere, watching your every step. There's a real magic to this place and it's for good reason it's known as one of the most beautiful nature reserves in the country. Information and tours: *West Tours (tel. 456 5111 | westtours.is).* *C–D 1–2*

STYKKISHÓLMUR

(C–D6) **This pretty town boasts a strikingly modern church and a long tradition as a fishing hub. Stykkishólmur was one of the German Hanseatic League's trading posts in the 16th century, together with Ísafjördur, Rif, Arnarstapi and Flatey.**

Today's population are rightly proud of their well-preserved old houses, which lend the little town its own special charm. You can take a ferry from Stykkishólmur to the south coast of the Westfjords.

SIGHTSEEING

VATNASAFN

The Library of Water is an installation by American artist Roni Horn: 24 glass tubes filled with water from Iceland's glaciers, their shimmering colours dictated by the light. Get the code for the door at the museum Norska Húsið at 5 Hafnargata. *Bókhlöðustigur 17 | libraryofwater.is*

SÚGANDISEY

This island is joined to the mainland by a causeway, thereby offering protection to the harbour. From here, you have a fine view of the islands scattered across the Breiðafjörður bay, while the many cosy hollows are perfect for romantics.

EATING & DRINKING

NARFEYRARSTOFA

There is a cosy *café (£)* on the ground floor of this pretty, old house and a *restaurant (££)* on the first floor. *Delicious local produce (including beer). Daily noon–10pm | Aðalgata 3 | tel. 533 1119 | narfeyrarstofa.is*

SJAVARPAKKHUSID

Fish as it should be: freshly caught, prepared and served. This 100-year-old house is situated directly on the harbour front, and you can watch the comings and goings while enjoying your meal. The fish is fabulous, but we particularly recommend the mussels and for dessert make sure to try the *skyr. Daily 6–11pm | Hafnargata 2 | tel. 438 1800 | sjavarpakkhusid.is | ££–£££*

WELLNESS

SUNDLAUG

Modern swimming pool complex with a special pool for length swimmers, plus a slide and hot pots. But the best thing about it is the water. With a pH value of 8.45 and high mineral content, the water has rejuvenating powers and is ideal for treating psoriasis and other skin conditions, or simply for relaxing. Some Icelanders are said to take the water home with them in bottles. *June–Aug Mon–Thu 7.05am–10pm, Fri 7.05am–7pm, Sat/Sun 10am–6pm, Sept–May Mon–Fri 7.05am–10pm, Sat/Sun 10am–5pm | admission 900 ISK | Borgarbraut 4 | tel. 433 8150*

AROUND STYKKISHÓLMUR

5 SNÆFELLSJÖKULL NATIONAL PARK ★

Entrance 82km west of Stykkishólmur, coastal tour by car 2–6 hrs

In the centre of the 167km² national park is the 1,446m-high volcanic peak, *Snæfellsjökull*. People believe that the mountain and its immediate surroundings generate a special kind of energy. The coast at the foot of the volcano is particularly fascinating. Far to the south, the rock pillars at *Lóndrangar* tower up out of the sea, inhabited by thousands of seabirds; to the west lies Dritvík Bay, once an important fishing port, today just a few ruined buildings. The black lava pebble beach at *Djúpalónssandur* is an attraction in itself. *B6–7*

6 FLATEY

37km north of Stykkishólmur in Breiðafjörður

With almost zero cars, old, well kept houses and true tranquillity, you'd be forgiven for thinking you'd stepped into another world. Today, the island in the Breiðafjörður is more of a summer stopover, but in the 19th century it was a major cultural centre. "Flat island" became famous due to the *Flateyarbók* manuscript, dating from the end of the 14th century, which describes, among other things, Leifur Eiríksson's voyage to America.

Today, only a few families still live here all year round, with most people coming just for the summer season. The painted ceiling in the small church has made it a particular hit.

INSIDER TIP
Painted church ceiling

The Baldur ferry travels to Flatey every day, from both the northwest coast and Stykkishólmur. Information and tickets from *Seatours (seatours.is)*. *E5 C5*

7 EIRÍKSSTAÐIR

85km east of Stykkishólmur, 1½ hrs by car

Watch your head! This is an impressive reconstruction of a longhouse from 1,000 years ago, where the son of Erik the Red – Leifur Eiríksson – was born. Tour guides dressed in medieval costume invite you inside and tell stories of old times. *20 June–Sept 10am–4pm | admission 2,500 ISK, children under 12 free | Route. 586 | leif.is | E6*

BORGARNES

(E8) **Calling all saga fans: this is the place for you! The first settler here was said to be Skallagrímur Kveldúlfsson, father of the famous skaldic poet Egil Skallagrímsson, hero of his own work, *Egil's Saga*. Admittedly, archaeological finds are yet to prove that Kveldúlfsson really did find his final resting place in what is now Borgarnes, but who's focusing on the details?**

Founded in 1867, modern Borganes is the economic powerhouse of western Iceland and plays a particularly important role in agricultural

THE VIKINGS

Real tough bad guys, legend has it, who roamed the known world, murdering and pillaging as they went. But this image doesn't tally with the reality of the average Icelandic Viking. They were actually farmers from Norway who refused to subject themselves to the authority of King Haraldur. Their search for suitable land to settle in away from his reach brought them to Iceland. Flóki Vilgerðarson set out back in 865 and landed on the northwest coast. He gave the new territory the name Ìsland ("ice land") because he was trapped here for two winters by the ice floes. Despite this hardly flattering designation, word of the land spread quickly, and large-scale settlement began in earnest from 874.

The west was much prized by the settlers for its rich pastureland and plentiful fishing grounds. A number of very rich farmers and *goðar* (leaders) lived here. Some of the best-known sagas are set in these parts: *Egil's Saga*, the *Laxdæla Saga* and others featuring Erik the Red have their origins in this region. It's not surprising, then, that in many places you can come across traces of these saga heroes, the real Icelandic Vikings.

A panoramic view of legendary Borgarnes

processing. The town's hot water supply comes from Iceland's largest hot spring, Deildartunguhver, 33km away. Despite its stunning location, the townscape seems rather sterile. Its charm lies in the fact that you stumble across traces of Egil's *Skallagrímssonar* everywhere.

SIGHTSEEING

SKALLAGRÍMSGARÐUR

This pretty park lies in the centre of town and is the site of the burial mound under which Egil's father, Skallagrímur Kvéldúlfsson, is said to lie. The first settler was laid to rest in the Viking tradition with his horse and weapons. Nearby, a relief shows Egil carrying his drowned son, Böðvar, whom he also buried under the burial mound, according to the saga.

LANDNÁMSSETUR

The best place to start your Egil discovery. The museum showcases the story of the settlement of Iceland, especially in the region around Borgarnes, as well *Egill's Saga*, across two exhibitions. Clever use of modern lighting design and good computer animation. *Daily 10am–5pm | admission 3,000 ISK, 6–12 years 1,000 ISK (for both exhibitions) | Brákarbraut 13–15 | landnam.is*

EATING & DRINKING

BÚÐARKLETTUR

Welcoming restaurant located in an old warehouse directly next to the Settlement Centre. Good regional food. *Daily 11.30am–9pm | Brákarbraut 13–15 | tel. 437 1600 | ££*

SPORT & ACTIVITIES

ESJA TRAVEL

A slightly different Icelandic experience for keen knitters. A four-day knitting course in small groups is held in Borgarnes.

INSIDER TIP **Knitting workshop**

Autumn in Hraunfossar: crystal-clear water, colourful vegetation and a dusting of snow

It takes you from sheep to scarf, and includes trips to sheep farms and wool-processing plants. *esjatravel.is*

HVÍTÁTRAVEL

Guided walking tour (in English) for groups on the trail of Egil. *June–Aug | 4,200 ISK 1½ hrs | starting at Landnámssetur Museum | tel. 661 7173*

AROUND BORGARNES

8 BORG Á MÝRUM

4km north of Borgarnes, 10 mins by car, 1 hr on foot

This site, a little to the north of Borgarnes, is where Skallagrímur Kvéldúlfsson built the farmstead where Egil was born. In front of the church, the sculpture *Snorratorrek* by Ásmundur Sveinsson represents Egil's lament for the death of his son, Böðvar. This expansively meditative place promises peace and escape. *E8*

9 DEILDARTUNGUHVER

37km east of Borgarnes, 45 mins by car

The biggest hot water spring in Iceland. At an incredible 100°C, the water supplies both Borganes and the area's many greenhouses. The supply point is right next to the spring.

Swim and relax to your heart's content in the waters of the Deildartunguhver spring at the *Krauma spa (daily 11am–9pm | admission 4,900 ISK | tel. 555 6066 | krauma.is)* in Reykholtsdalur. The six

pools, all different sizes, are each a different temperature. A must is the cold water pool (5–8 °C) – it will get your circulation going in no time! *F7*

10 HRAUNFOSSAR

55km east of Borgarnes, 50 mins by car

A group of waterfalls known as the "Lava Falls" spread over a distance of a kilometre in the *Hallmundarhraun* lava field. The sight of the crystal-clear water flowing into the milky glacial water of the Hvítá river below is a beautiful one. This watery spectacle is particularly stunning in September, when the vegetation glows in autumnal hues. *F–G7*

INSIDER TIP **Waterfalls and autumn colours**

11 HÚSAFELL

68km west of Borgarnes, 1 hr by car

This sheltered location is one of Icelanders' favourite places to head to at weekends. Its plentiful coverage of trees and host of hiking paths mean the area has plenty of leisure options, and the added benefit of being within easy reach of the Highlands. In the more distant past, the original Húsafell farmstead was an important supply point for travellers en route from north to south. Near the old priest's house you'll find several rocks and lava stones with faces carved into them. The artist Páll Guðmundsson lives on site – his studio is in the tower. If he's in the mood, he'll happily show you his other works. Otherwise, you can see more at *Hotel Húsafell*.

INSIDER TIP **Studio visit**

Enjoy a leisurely dip in the local swimming pool or head out for an exciting excursion to the new natural pool at the heart of the lava landscape, the *Húsafell Canyon Baths (all year round | 9,900 ISK, includes tour, transport and towel | husafell.com/activities/husafell-canon-baths). F7*

WHERE TO SLEEP IN THE WEST

A SOLITARY SEA VIEW

Live the dream of the lonely lighthouse keeper in *Hornbjargsviti (D1)* and stay in the lighthouse at Hornstrandir. Basic, no-frills accommodation with stunning views of the sea and blossoming meadows. The next accommodation is 60km away as the crow flies! *fi.is | £*

THE HIGHLANDS

FIFTY SHADES OF GREY – FROM LAVA TO GRAVEL

It's home to elves, trolls and giants, who hide behind boulders and in green oases and play with the mountains like building blocks, throwing them into the vast plains. The largely uninhabited (by humans, at least) Highland region is Iceland at its most primal and breathtaking, a landscape fashioned by volcanic activity and ice. The Hofsjökull and Langjökull glaciers and monumental table mountains, such as the Herðubreið, emerge from grey-brown plains, dotted with colourful patches of vegetation.

Landmannalaugar: hot springs and colourful rocks

For centuries, the Highland routes were the main connection between north and south. Travellers would be relieved to finally reach their home farm, as these routes were not without their dangers. Numerous outlaws had retreated into the inhospitable Highlands and survived by means of highway robbery. The name of the huge, forbidding lava desert *Ódáðahraun* – which means something like "Evil Deeds Lava" – hints at this. Today, the Highlands are a challenge for off-road drivers, mountain bikers, hikers and adventurers.

THE HIGHLANDS

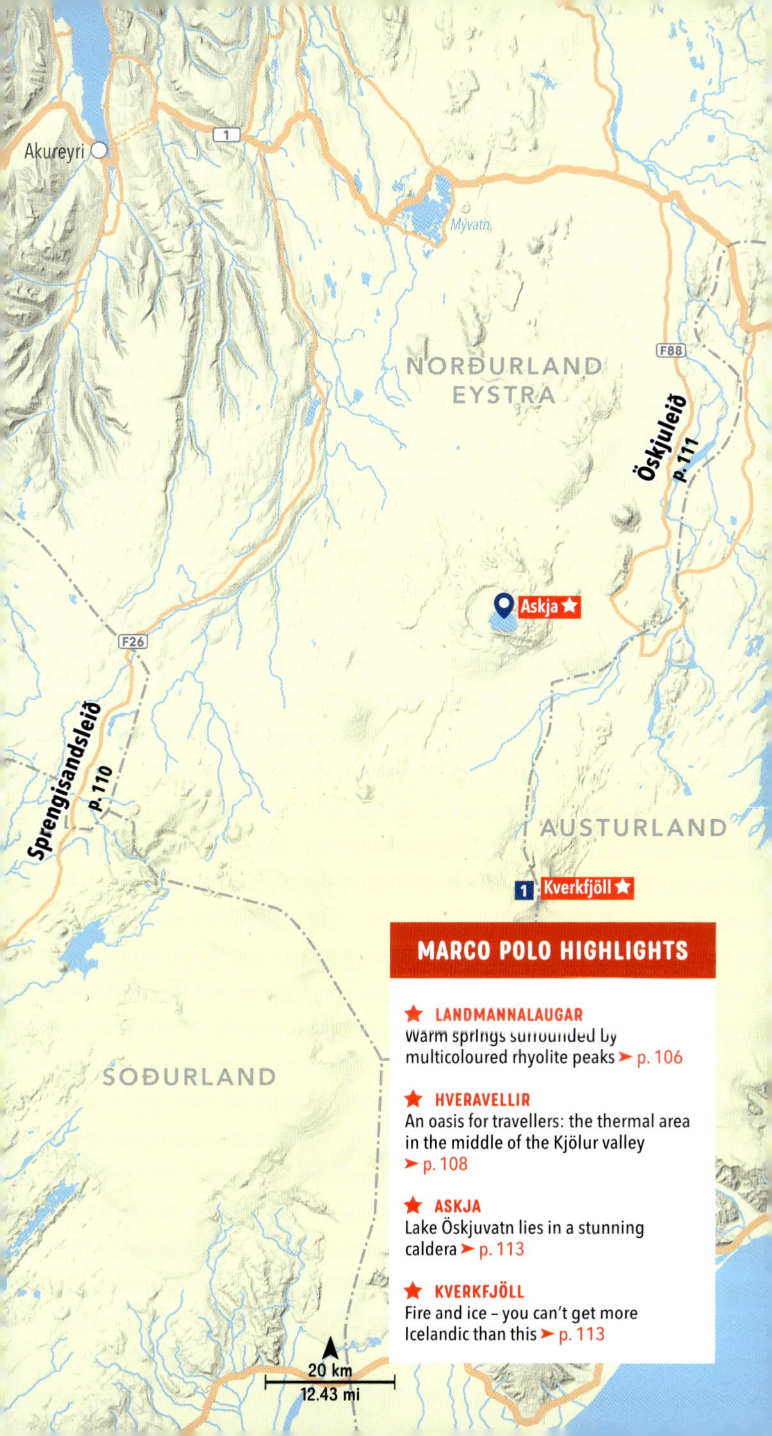

MARCO POLO HIGHLIGHTS

★ **LANDMANNALAUGAR**
Warm springs surrounded by multicoloured rhyolite peaks ➤ p. 106

★ **HVERAVELLIR**
An oasis for travellers: the thermal area in the middle of the Kjölur valley ➤ p. 108

★ **ASKJA**
Lake Öskjuvatn lies in a stunning caldera ➤ p. 113

★ **KVERKFJÖLL**
Fire and ice – you can't get more Icelandic than this ➤ p. 113

FJALLABAKS LEIÐ NYRÐI

The "Northern Trail Behind the Mountains" runs from west to east and was an essential link for centuries.

The roughly 84km-long road (Route F 208) begins in the northwest near the Sigalda power plant on the *Hrauneyalón lake (🕮 J9)* and ends in the southeast near *Búland (🕮 K11)*, where it joins Route. 208. Alternatively, in the west, follow the Landmannaleið running south for 47km (Route F 225). The trail climbs in some places to heights of between 500m and 1,000m and leads through a bizarre, yet beautiful, landscape. To the north of the Hekla volcano, the *Sölvahraun* lava field, with its crevasses and craters cloaked in black ash, presents an apocalyptic picture.

To the east of the lava fields around Hekla is Iceland's largest area of rhyolite deposits, covering around 400km². Rhyolite is a siliceous volcanic rock, notable for its reddish or greenish colour.

SIGHTSEEING

LANDMANNALAUGAR ★

More than any other place in Iceland, Landmannalaugar is intrinsically linked to its soothing hot springs. In the "Country People's Warm Springs", the farmers of past centuries used to recuperate from the arduous task of driving their sheep back down the mountains. Today, they are possibly Iceland's best-known geothermal waters, surrounded by rhyolite peaks that light up in a mind-blowing multitude of colours that vary with the position of the sun and air humidity. From *Bláhnúkur* (943m) – which gets its name from its blue-green rock – you can look across to the vast obsidian lava field *Laugahraun*, a labyrinthine expanse of black lava formations, some 40m high. *🕮 J10*

ELDGJÁ

Translated as "Fire Gorge", the valley extends for 40km from the Uxatindar peak as far as the edge of the Myrdalsjokull glacier in the southwest. It looks particularly breathtaking near *Gjátindur* (935m), where it is over 200m deep and up to 600m wide. The oldest lava is around 5,000 years old and new layers and currents were added over the years. Some of the lava flows reached as far as the Myrdalssandur glacial outwash plain in southern Iceland. The southwesterly section of the Eldgja rift consists of a row of craters. This ancient, primeval landscape manages to be both strange and enchanting at the same time. *🕮 K10*

KALDIDALUR

(🕮 F–G 7–8) **Route F 550, the Kaldidalsvegur Route, is only 40km long and runs from Húsafell (see p. 101) as far as Route 52 near Þingvellir, past two glaciers,**

Langjökull and Þórisjökull in the east, and the 1,198m-high glacial peak, Ok, in the west. Nestled in among the ice, it's easy to see where the place gets its name: *Kaldidalur* means "Cold Valley".

The route climbs to around 700m in some places. The real beauty of the route lies in the views of the glaciers, combined with the sight of a number of landmark peaks, such as *Prestahnúkur* (1,069m) which consists of greenish rhyolite rock.

SIGHTSEEING

LAVA CAVES

The *Surtshellir* lava cave near Húsafell is the largest in the country at 1.6km in length. Back in the tenth century, people used to live here. Like the *Stefánshellir* cave, it is located in the *Hallmundarhraun* lava flow, which can be found north of the village on Route 518. You can reach the track to the cave by car; the route is signposted and there is even a car park. The cave is relatively accessible, but a torch and good walking boots are important. Winter snow makes for an even more atmospheric experience, but of course a trickier one, too. Book a tour for an ultimate cave experience which leads you through a lava tube and down into the depths of the cave. It takes you inside the *Víðgelmir* lava cave, with magnificent lava formations in varying colours that create a magical underground world. *Fljótstunga | from 1½hrs | 7,000 ISK, children 7–15 3,800 ISK | thecave.is | G7*

LANGJÖKULL

Iceland's second largest glacier welcomes you to step inside. An artificial tunnel leads you into the ice, from

The thermal springs at Landmannalaugar are perfect for a dip

where you can take a good look at the ice layers and experience the world inside an ice cap *(approx. 4hrs from Húsafell | 22,200 ISK)*. You can also link the glacier and lava caves. The most exciting adventure consists of the ice tunnel and a snowmobile ride on the glacier *(3–4 hrs from Húsafell | from 34,990 ISK)*. intotheglacier.is

From the east side of Langjökull, you can take to the ice with tour operators *Mountaineers of Iceland*. Since winter 2018, there has been the most spectacular new highlight: the incredible blue ice cave. You can opt for the combined tour of cave visit plus snowmobile ride all year round. *Info: Köllunarklettsvegur 2, 104 Reykjavík | base camp: Skálpanes on Route F 336 | 31,000 ISK | tel. 580 9900 | mountaineers.is | ▯ G–H 7–8*

INSIDER TIP **Into the blue**

KJALVEGUR

The spectacular Highland route, Kjalvegur (Route F 35, hire cars not allowed), leads from *Gullfoss* in southern Iceland *(▯ H9)* 165km northwards to the Blanda power plant above *Blöndulón* lake *(▯ H6)*.

The old route led from one bishopric to another and Þingvellir is relatively close by, too. Probably the most impressive section of the journey in scenic terms runs through the *Kjölur* valley, a deserted lava and gravel plain at an altitude of almost 700m between the Langjökull and Hofsjökull glaciers. Although the journey today is safe and comfortable, it was a far more perilous affair many years ago. The route originally ran further west through the Kjalhraun, but it was re-routed in the wake of a tragic accident in 1780. Four people, together with 180 sheep and 16 horses, died here in a snow storm. To this day, the *Beinahóll* hill, which you can reach via a track, is strewn with animal bones. In this vast expanse of desert terrain, there is no shelter against wind and weather for miles.

INSIDER TIP **Remnants of a tragedy**

SIGHTSEEING

KERLINGARFJÖLL

The name Kerlingarfjöll means "Woman's Mountain" because it is said that one of the rocks is a female troll set in stone. The myriad colours of the rhyolite mountain range towering over the Kjölur plain are visible for miles around. The highest peaks, Snækollur (1,477m), Loðmundur (1,432m) and Mænir (1,355m) are partially covered with ice caps. In some of the multicoloured, glistening valleys, solfataras make for a steaming, spluttering spectacle. This is the place to experience Iceland in miniature: fire and ice side by side. Plus, once you've finished hiking for the day, it would be rude not to relax in the hot spring by the river! *▯ J8*

HVERAVELLIR ★

The hot springs of Hveravellir must have been a sight for sore eyes when

Bláhver, or the "blue spring", in Hveravellir is an other-worldly sight

riders finally reached them in years gone by. The thermal area lies in the middle of the Kjölur plain, on the northern edge of the Kjalhraun. Travellers in the Middle Ages enjoyed bathing in the hot springs, which they also used for cooking! There are around 20 bubbling springs; some of them are stunningly beautiful. *Bláhver*, the 7m-wide "Blue Spring", is characterised by sinter deposits and turquoise-to-aquamarine blue water. The ultimate picture-postcard image is surely *Fagrihver*, the "Beautiful Spring", with its clear, shimmering turquoise waters. Today, you can still find a hot pot at one of the cabins; after all, contemporary travellers are just as fond of the warming experience. *J7*

EYVINDARHELLIR

Iceland's most famous outlaw, Fjalla Eyvindur, lived in Hveravellir for some time with his wife Halla. You can still see their lava cave, Eyvindarhellir, in the nearby Kjalhraun lava field. The pair are said to have dunked their meat, from stolen sheep of course, directly into the spring water of nearby Eyvindarhver for cooking, going on to survive like this in the Highlands for 20 years. The hike on the signposted trail from Hveravellir takes an hour. *J*

SPORT & ACTIVITIES

You need a rucksack, tent, proper hiking maps and enough food for several days and it is time for the adventure to begin! Think solitude, exciting routes, wading through rivers and nature in its purest form. Peak after peak beckons, and you will even get the chance to cross some glaciers. Luckily, plenty of campsites are available, making it the ideal hike even for beginners (see p. 118, Discovery Tour 2).

SPRENGI SANDSLEIÐ

The 250km-long Sprengisandsleið Route *(🕮 26)* **runs from the Mýri farm in the north** *(🕮 M5)* **down to the Þjórsárdalur valley in the south** *(🕮 H–J9)*. **The barren, stony Sprengisandur desert in the middle of the route is characterised by two glaciers: Vatnajökull and Hofsjökull.**

Iceland's largest stone desert stretches from Hofsjökull to the Tungnafellsjökull glaciers, over 70km from north to south. Only isolated mountains line the route to Nýidalur, including Þveralda (728m), which gives an incredible view of the Hágöngur rhyolite mountains. The pink, stemless cinquefoil flowers are a welcome splash of colour in this seemingly infinite expanse of brown and grey.

In the Middle Ages, this ancient north–south route was mainly used by the Bishop of Skálholt as he travelled to eastern Iceland. Later, in the 18th and 19th centuries, it was rediscovered as a way to traverse the country, and yet it never lost its eerie air, especially as the northern section runs right past the Ódáðahraun desert.

The name, which also designates the route, only came into use in the 18th century. In the Middle Ages, it was simply known as Sandur (sand). The word *sprengir* derives from the verb *sprengja* (to tire out). The Sprengisandur desert was not only feared because of its sandstorms and highwaymen, but also because the individual grazing grounds were more than a day's ride apart. Not surprisingly, riders were keen to reach their destination by nightfall.

The Aldeyjarfoss waterfall plunges 20m into a ravine

SIGHTSEEING

STÖNG

Once a large settlement with 20 farmsteads in the fertile Þjórsárdalur valley, Stöng was buried under white volcanic ash in 1104 during one of Hekla's eruptions. Only two farms are left standing today, even though the valley is green once again. The indoor ruins can be visited all year round. *H9*

HOFSJÖKULL

The third-largest glacier in the country covers an area of 995km². Its white cap can be seen from miles away and measures up to 1,760m. It may appear peaceful, but below the summit a volcano slumbers. On the southeast periphery of the glacier is the *Þjórsárver* Nature Reserve, a swampy area with moorland vegetation, lakes and ponds. Around 11,000 pairs of pink-footed goose nest and rear their young here. *J–K7*

NÝIDALUR

This valley on the southern side of the Tungnafellsjökull glacier is surprisingly green, with flowering meadows, and at 800m above sea level quite possibly the highest one in the country. You can easily explore the region from here, for example the geothermal area south of the Tungnafellsjökull on the *Eggja* mountain (1,271m). *L7*

ALDEYJARFOSS

The picturesque Aldeyjarfoss waterfall forms the end point of the Sprengisandsleið, where the Skálfandafljót river churns through a narrow passage and into a 20m deep pool in a canyon lined with beautiful basalt column formations. These 4,500-year old columns originate from an eruption of the Trölladyngja volcano on the northern edge of Vatnajökull. *M5*

ÖSKJULEIÐ

(O4–6) **They say the road to Heaven leads through Hell, and you could certainly say the same of this route** *(88)*, **which leads through Ódáðahraun.**

The name alone isn't exactly comforting! A "Desert of Evil Deeds"? What on earth awaits? Well, an expanse of over 4,550km² of lava, stretching between the rivers Skálfandafljót and Jökulsá á Fjöllum. Ódáðahraun is the

SUPER JEEPS

Four-wheel-drive vehicles in Iceland are real eye-catchers; with their 44-inch tyres and correspondingly modified, wide bodywork, they look rather intimidating. But when you drive along one of the Highland trails yourself, you'll wish you could trade your vehicle for one of these super jeeps. They positively glide over lava, stones and all uneven surfaces. In winter, their strengths come to the fore, as their thick tyres effortlessly negotiate the snowy surface. Try one for yourself: trips are offered by several tour operators.

This ice cave in the Kverkjökull glacier was formed by meltwater

largest contiguous area of lava in Iceland. It dates back 5,000 years, and sand, gravel and monolithic table mountains of palagonite give it its distinctive appearance: black, menacing, dismal and arid. Rainfall seeps away so quickly that plants are unable to make use of the moisture. Only at the edges of the lava desert do green and fruitful oases such as *Herðubreiðarlindir* appear, where groundwater emerges in small springs. Öskjuleið leads over 88km as far as the northern edge of the Vatnajökull and the famous Askja caldera.

SIGHTSEEING

HERÐUBREIÐARLINDIR

Lush greenery and over 100 species of plant can be seen in this oasis, which draws its water from the Lindaá river. Herðubreiðarfriðland has been a nature reserve since 1974 and is now part of Vatnajökull National Park. After the former spectacle in grey, the landscape transforms into a green paradise; after the silence of the lava wastelands, the vibrant sound of birdsong is awe-inspiring. Some 30 species, most commonly the snow bunting, thrive here among the plants and insects. The charms of this oasis weren't lost on outlaw Fjalla Eyvindur, who sheltered here one harsh winter. You can still see his small cave today.

Herðubreiðarlindir takes its name from the formidable *Herðubreið* mountain (1,682m), formed during an eruption under the 1,000m-thick ice crust during the last Ice Age. The ascent is difficult due to the loose covering of scree, but the view from the top is overwhelming. A path leads from the oasis towards the mountain through a beautiful lava landscape, where the characteristic *pahoehoe* (or knitted) lava formations are particularly well defined. 🕮 O6

INSIDER TIP
Lava formations

ASKJA ★

In the heart of the Dyngjufjöll range, a central volcanic system which has been active for hundreds of thousands of years, lies this natural monument: the *Askja* caldera with its dazzlingly blue lake, *Öskjuvatn*. The crater was formed around 6,000 years ago and is almost circular, 8km in diameter. Its sides are between 200m and 400m high and are precipitously steep in places. Still, hiking in the middle of a volcano is not without its charms. After all, where else can you do that?

The best view of the Askja is from *Þorvaldstindur* (1,510m) on the southern edge of Dyngjufjöll. The *Öskjuvatn* lake, 217m deep, was the result of a massive eruption in 1875. Ash buried 16 farms and 10,000km² of land. But the depths of the lake hide a dark secret. Back in 1907, geologist Walther von Knebel and painter Max Rudolff disappeared while exploring the lake. Nobody knows that became of them … and their bodies were never found.

On the northern edge of the lake lies the crater lake *Víti*, with its milky, green-blue water. The brave descend to bathe in its pleasantly warm temperatures, but the foul odour rising from the water is far less inviting! 🕮 N6

HÓLUHRAUN

This is Iceland's youngest lava. The *Bárðarbunga* volcano on the northwest edge of the Vatnjökull erupted from August 2014 until February 2015. You can walk across parts of this newly created, 85km² sharp-edged lava field on paths marked by signs. 🕮 N7

AROUND ÖSKJULEIÐ

1 KVERKFJÖLL ★

45km south of the Askja, 1½–2 hrs by car on jeep tracks

The mountain range on the northern edge of the Vatnajökull is a volcanic system with an ice-filled caldera. The glacier tongue *Kverkjökull* pushes its way out of a north-facing opening. One of Iceland's largest geothermal areas lies on the western flank of the range: *Hveradalur*. Here, a series of fascinating ice caves and tunnels have been carved out underneath the glacier. 🕮 N8

WHERE TO SLEEP IN THE HIGHLANDS

COUNTRYSIDE CAMPING

The cosiest campsite in the Highlands has to be the one at *Herðubreiðarlindir*. Birdsong, babbling brooks and fresh blooms abound. Find your own sheltered corner – probably some distance from the lodge and service building for peace and quiet. *ffa.is* | £

DISCOVERY TOURS

Want to get under the skin of this country? Then our discovery tours are the ideal guide – they provide advice on which sights to visit, tips on where to stop for that perfect holiday snap, a choice of the best places to eat and drink, and suggestions for fun activities.

1 THE GOLDEN CIRCLE: NATURE, CULTURE AND A WHOLE LOT OF HISTORY

- Dive between continental plates
- Lose yourself in the mist of hot springs
- Snack on greenhouse treasures

Start: Reykjavík
Finish: Reykjavík

Distance: 280km
Duration: 3 days (total driving time 7 hours)

Costs: around £770/2 people.
Book hotel rooms in advance in the summer months.
Pay attention to weather reports *(vedur.is)*. Book diving tour in advance *(adventure.is)*.

Don't forget your waterproofs when visiting the Gulfoss waterfall!

FROM NOBEL PRIZE WINNERS TO NATIONAL PARKS

Take the four-lane Route 1 from ❶ **Reykjavík** ➤ **p. 38** *heading north to Mosfellsbær.* You won't see much more than houses and large shops as one place flows into the next. After this built-up area, just as you leave the town, turn off on to Route 36, the Þingvallavegur. There you'll find agricultural land with meadows, farms and horses galore. After a few kilometres, you will come to ❷ **Gljúfrasteinn** *(June–Aug daily 10am–5pm | gljufrasteinn.is),* the former home of the Nobel Prize winning author Halldór Laxness, who lived here with his family after 1945. His white Jaguar is sometimes parked outside. The house is full of history and stories – both by and about him. When you are up on the plateau of Mosfellsheiði, you'll be able to see Iceland's largest lake, ❸ **Þingvallavatn** ➤ **p. 53**, and the adjoining national park ❹ **Þingvellir** ➤ **p. 52**. The Hakið observation point at the **Information Centre** offers a sweeping view into the Highlands complete with impressive volcanoes and glaciers. Numerous signposted trails lead from here to **Lögberg**, through the **Almannagjá** and further on to **Öxará waterfall**. En route, you will see former execution sites. A snorkelling or diving

DAY 1

❶ **Reykjavík**

21km 20 mins

❷ **Gljúfrasteinn**

20km 15 mins

❸ **Þingvallavatn**

11km 25 mins

❹ **Þingvellir**

32.5km 2.5 hrs

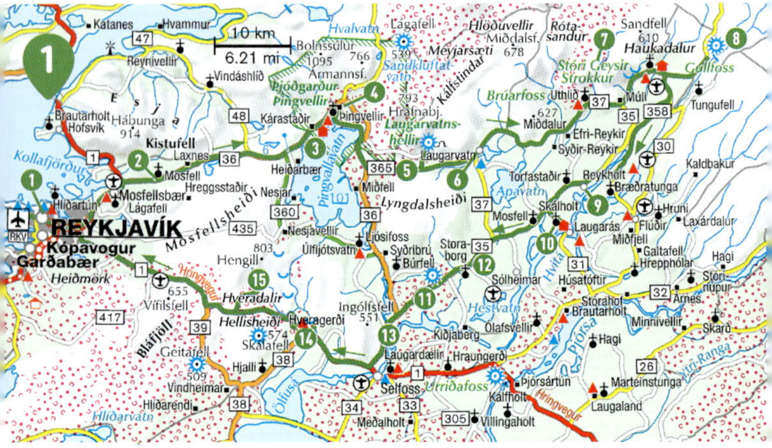

5 Laugarvatnshellir

9.5km 15 mins

6 Laugarvatn

excursion in the **Sílfra Rift ➤ p. 53** is a spectacular way to get acquainted with the lake and the geology of the park that sits between two continental plates.

FROM HOLIDAY HOMES TO LAVA CAVES

The route continues on through a scrub forest near the lake. Of course, in Iceland, wherever there are trees, there are also holiday homes (or summer houses, as they're known), and **Þingvallavatn** is a hugely popular spot. You'll *then head towards Laugarvatn via Route 365*. You'll drive over the foothills of an extinct shield volcano in a landscape full of different kinds of lava. *Halfway to the next destination*, you'll come across the two caves of **5 Laugarvatnshellir**, which were still inhabited at the beginning of the 20th century! Join a guided tour of the caves *(thecavepeople.is)* to hear fascinating stories about them. The village of **6 Laugarvatn**, with its forests and summer houses, is a popular choice among Reykjavík's locals for a short getaway during the summer months. The hot springs are mostly used to heat greenhouses and, of course, hot pots. The **Golden Circle Apartments** *(goldencircleapartments.is)* are located close to the lake and the wonderful hot pots of the nearby **Fontana Spa** *(fontana.is)* are an ideal place for a relaxing stay. You can get a 10% discount here if you show your apartment key.

INTO THE WORLD OF GEYSERS

The next stops are all about water. *Head northeast on Route 37 and Routen35* into the thermal geyser area around Haukadalur – which you can see from afar thanks to the fountain of water spewed by the ❼ Strokkur geyser ➤ p. 61. It's well worth a visit, but depending on the wind direction you'll need to watch where you stand if you don't want to find yourself soaked by the geyser's spray! Your only option then is a quick jump out of its path.

Continue driving to the impressive waterfall ❽ Gullfoss ➤ p. 61. Several paths will take you near the cascades. Once at the top, you walk on wood and there are plenty of slippery paths to the spray mist at the bottom for water lovers. *Return to the geyser area and continue driving south.* The small village of ❾ Reykholt ➤ p. 60 is home to numerous greenhouses heated with the steaming hot water – you can see the vapour rising from the ground. Pay attention to the signs on the side of the road for places to buy fresh tomatoes and strawberries.

INSIDER TIP
Fresh fruit and vegetables

After so much nature, take a quick detour into history. *A few kilometres further on, Route 31 branches off* to the bishop's seat of ❿ Skálholt, which was the cultural centre of Iceland from the Middle Ages into the 19th century. Treat yourself to some homemade cake in the school building before heading *southwards on Route 35. After 10km,* you will come to a 3,000-year-old and 55m-deep explosion crater filled with water on your left called ⓫ Kerið. *Then drive back a few kilometres on Route 35* to your cosy accommodation, ⓬ Cottages Minniborgir *(minniborgir.is).* Wind down for the evening with a dip in a hot pot and dinner made with local ingredients.

FROM FIRST SETTLER TO GEOTHERMAL ENERGY

Shortly before you come to the Ring Road, leading to Reykjavík, stop briefly at ⓭ Fjallstún at the foot of the Ingólfsfjall, supposedly the site where the first settler of Iceland, Ingólfur Arnarson, spent his first winter. You

DAY 2
30km 50 mins
❼ Strokkur
10.5km 15 mins
❽ Gullfoss
28km 30 mins
❾ Reykholt
8.5km 10 mins
❿ Skálholt
23.5km 20 mins
⓫ Kerið
8km 7 mins
⓬ Cottages Minniborgir

DAY 3
9km 10 mins
⓭ Fjallstún
14km 10 mins

⑭ Hveragerði
19.5km 15 mins
⑮ Hellisheiði
32km 30 mins
① Reykjavík

should also stop at ⑭ **Hveragerði** ➤ p. 58 to visit the geothermal field, go for a spa treatment or hike to the hot springs. The **exhibition** in the shopping centre shows the damage caused by the earthquake in 2008. At the geothermal power plant ⑮ **Hellisheiði** *(daily 9am–5pm | on.is)*, you can learn about the uses of geothermal energy as well as the history of the region with its many legends *before you make your way back to* ① **Reykjavík** ➤ p. 38.

② SKIRTING THE GLACIER: KJALVEGUR

- ➤ Breathtaking views of peaks and glaciers
- ➤ Along and up the glacier
- ➤ Hot pot for tired feet at the end of your trip

Start: Hvítarvatn lake

Finish: Hveravellir

Distance: 51km

Duration: 4 days (total walking time 12 hours)

Difficulty: easy

Costs: bus tickets around £85/person, cabins approx. £40/person per night.
What to pack: tent, sleeping bag etc; backpack; food and drink; trail maps and/or GPS.
Book and pay for cabins (self-catering) in advance *(fi.is)*; buses run daily in summer from Reykjavík and Akureyri over the Kjölur mountain track. When you board the bus, tell the driver that you want to get off at Hvítárnes.

DAY 1
① "Hvítarvatn"
8.5km 2 hrs
② Hvítárnes lodge

STUNNING GLACIAL VIEWS FROM THE CABIN

This route begins at the sign for ① **"Hvítarvatn"** on the Kjölur jeep track, *where you'll get off the bus and walk to the* ② **Hvítárnes lodge**. This red-roofed lodge is located on Hvítárvatn lake on the eastern edge of the Langjökull. Today, the track to the lodge has a bridge

Warm water in a wild landscape

but back in 1930, when it was built, all the materials had to be transported by packhorse. From here you can see the beautiful Nyrðriskriðjökull glacier – and how much it has retreated. Next to the lodge you will see the ruins of a farm likely destroyed in the Hekla eruption of 1104. Today, the lush vegetation draws in songbirds while the lake is a much-loved spot for ducks and geese

RICH VEGETATION ON HILLS AND MOUNTAINS

DAY 2

On the morning of the second day, get your bearings by following the stone cairns to the east of the lodge that mark the way to the old Kjalvegur road ➤ p. 108. *The path leading northeast along the Fúlakvísl river is easy to follow.* The rich vegetation surrounding the ❸ **Hrefnubuðir** tuff (volcanic rock) mound comes as a surprise, and there are even birch trees growing here at an elevation 400–500m. Take a break for a moment and let your gaze wander: the Hrútfell table mountain

5.5km 2 hrs

❸ Hrefnubuðir

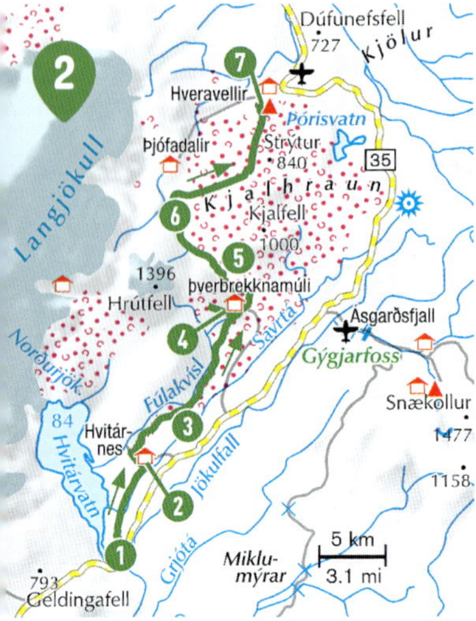

(1,410m) towers above you, while the Kerlingarfjöll mountains ➤ p. 108 rise up to the east. *Once you have crossed the Þverbrekknaver marsh, cross the bridge over the river and follow the signposts to* ❹ **Þverbrekknamúli**. Pretty tent pitches are situated along the stream not far from the **lodge**. How does a day trip to the glacier sound? Your destination is the **Fjallkirkja** rock formation on the Langjökull, about 15km away from here. Great views are included for free.

10km 2.5 hrs

❹ **Þverbrekknamúli**

7km 1.5 hrs

❺ **Hlaupin**

DAY 3

5.5km 1 hr 20 mins

❻ **Þjófadalir**

DAY 4

14.5km 3.5 hrs

❼ **Hveravellir**

IN THE VALLEY OF THIEVES

Head back to the bridge and continue along the old Kjalvegur. Since you will not cross any more rivers or streams today, make sure to stock up before you go. Just so you know, freshly drawn Icelandic water is incredible. *At first, the trail runs parallel to the small Fúlakvísl river,* which flows into a narrow canyon. *Then it runs to the east of Múli hill* before coming to the narrow ❺ **Hlaupin** canyon, where the Fúlakvísl once again tumbles through the lava rock. *Keep your bearings as you walk north by heading towards Þjófafell (960m).* You'll finally reach water again at the green banks of the Þjófadalaá stream. The stream leads into the valley of ❻ **Þjófadalir** to the west of the mountain, which is home to the next **lodge**. In days gone by, the secluded valley was a hideaway for highwaymen, earning its name as "Thieves' Valley".

INSIDER TIP
Pure water

BACK TO CIVILISATION

Today you start with a hike to *Þröskuldur Pass, where you will come across the jeep route F 735 to* ❼ **Hveravellir** ➤ p. 108, where you can recover from the hike with a bath in the thermal spring water! Plus, there's no need to cook for yourself as can visit the small **cafeteria**. A lodge and campsite are also available. Fancy another tour?

❸ ÖSKJULEIÐ: THE GREY-GREEN CHALLENGE

- Cross the black and grey lava desert of Ódáðahraun
- An adventurous journey through rivers and oases
- Hike over young lava

Mývatn

Holuhraun

170km

2 days (total driving time 5 hours)

Costs: around £350/2 people incl. jeep rental, petrol and accommodation.
What to pack: tent, sleeping bag, etc., food and drink.
Book and pay for cabins in advance *(fi.is)*. Pay attention to weather reports *(vedur.is)*: do not travel when storm warnings have been issued! Be sure to wear hiking boots. Try to only ford waterways together with other vehicles. It is best to see how and where others are crossing, as the deepest channels are usually not the best. In the water, steer against the current. The earlier you start in the day, the lower the water levels in the rivers.

ACROSS THE FIRST RIVER TO THE NATURE RESERVE

Start from ❶ Mývatn lake ➤ p. 82. *The F 88 jeep track (also known as Öskjuleið) begins about 40km to the east*. You'll soon come across the ❷ Hrossaborg crater, whose partially collapsed rim towers up 40m – if you want to, you can climb to the top for a view of the lava landscape. *Continue driving, parallel to the Jökulsá á Fjöllum glacial river*. The river begins at the Vatnajökull, which you will mostly only hear along this route. *Ford for the first time across the* ❸ Grafarlandaá river, which marks the boundary of a nature conservation area extending as far as Herðubreiðarlindir and the Vatnajökull National Park. Before you reach this pretty

DAY 1
❶ Mývatn
36km 25 mins
❷ Hrossaborg
38.5km 1 hr 20 mins
❸ Grafarlandaá river
20km 20 mins

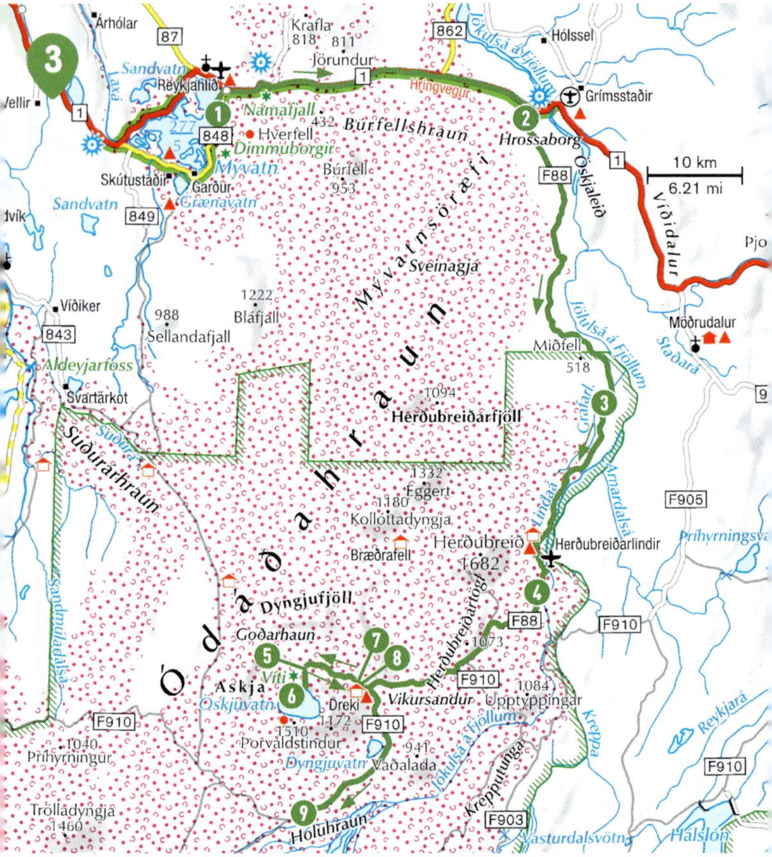

spot, with its bubbling streams and rich vegetation, *you will need to cross the Lindaá river.*

4 Herðubreiðarlindir

At the oasis of **4 Herðubreiðarlindir ➤ p. 112**, you should stop and head to the nearby lava field formed by a pahoehoe lava flow. The resulting rock formation resembles parallel rows of ropes; it was created when layers of thin, low-gas lava are successively shoved together. Take a look at the spot where Iceland's legendary outlaw, Fjalla-Eyvindur ("Eyvindur from the Mountains"), supposedly spent the winter of 1774/75.

TRAIN FOR THE MOON LANDING

The journey continues past the 8km-long tuff ridge Herðubreiðartögl (1,059m), south of Herðubreið mountain. The ground here consists largely of pale pumice formations, whose ash is carried for hundreds of kilometres by the stormy winds. The next destination is the Dyngjufjöll volcano and its caldera Askja ➤ p. 113. On the northern rim of the caldera, you will find the explosion crater ❺ Víti and the milky water of ❻ Öskjuvatn lake in the centre. *Return to the car park and head on back to the camping pitch at the lodge* ❼ Dreki, where you can spend the night. By the way, the lava along the way was used as a training site for astronauts in 1968 ahead of the 1969 moon landing.

44km 1.5 hrs

❺ Víti

1km 15 mins

❻ Öskjuvatn

10.5km 50 mins

❼ Dreki

It's worth the effort of an evening to walk through the ❽ Drekagil gorge, with its bizarre lava formations resembling dragons' heads. At the end is a magnificent waterfall. *The entrance to the gorge lies behind Dreki lodge.*

INSIDER TIP
Wonderful waterfall

300m 5 mins

❽ Drekagil

FINISH WITH SOME NEW MONSTERS

Depart Dreki heading south on the F 910 until you come to the "new lava" of ❾ Hóluhraun ➤ p. 113. It was spewed when the Báðarbunga volcano erupted for eight months until early 2015. Signs indicate the areas of the lava field where you are permitted to walk. The rock is sharp-edged and wildly upturned, a little monster seemingly lurking at every turn.

DAY 2

19km 30 mins

❾ Hóluhraun

If you have time, it's worth hiking around the caldera. Otherwise, *take the road to head back* out of the lava desert.

GOOD TO KNOW

HOLIDAY BASICS

ARRIVAL

GETTING THERE

Plenty of airlines offer flights to Iceland. Book early and you'll find offers for the summer, although it is obviously generally cheaper in the low season. Icelandair *(icelandair.is)*, the national carrier, flies from London. The price system is rather complicated, but it is possible to book reasonably priced flights by doing so early and flying outside the high season in summer. Be sure to compare offers from other airlines. The second Icelandic airline is WOW Air *(wowair.com)*, which also departs from London as well as Edinburgh, Bristol, Cork and Dublin. Flights are generally cheaper. Budget carrier Easyjet offers connections from London, Bristol, Edinburgh, Manchester and Belfast *(easyjet.com)*. KLM *(klm.com)* flies from New York direct to Reykjavík, the trip taking around six hours. Look on the Keflavík Airport website *(kefairport.is)* for an up-to-date list of other carriers currently serving Reykjavík; in recent years these have been known to change frequently.

On arrival, it's well worth a visit to duty free. Prices are generally lower than outside the airport and many Icelanders are sure to stop here too when returning from abroad. **INSIDER TIP Duty-free goods** Whether you want alcohol, perfume, tobacco, sweets, DVDs or computer games you'll find it here.

Buses run from Keflavík to the BSI bus station in Reykjavík (45 minutes), where you can transfer to other bus lines. Tickets can be purchased online *(re.is/flybus* and *airportdirect.is)* or at the airport. There are shuttles to hotels and hostels from the BSI bus station.

It's hard to keep your eyes on the road when the view is as good as this

TIME ZONE

Iceland observes Greenwich Mean Time (GMT) year round, so there's no time difference with the UK in winter. In summer, the UK is an hour ahead.

You can take the *Norröna* ferry, operated by *Smyril Line*, to travel from Hirtshals (Denmark) to Seyðisfjorður, with a stay in the Faroe Islands on the way. There are weekly departures in the low season (none from end November to mid-March), and twice weekly departures in summer. You can take your car, bike or motorbike. *smyril-line.com*

ENTRY REQUIREMENTS

For travellers from Schengen countries, there is no passport control; others will, of course, be checked as normal. If you are bringing your own vehicle into Iceland, you must carry your passport, vehicle registration documents, proof of valid insurance cover ("green card") and your driving licence. Drivers from the UK, US, Canada, Australia, New Zealand and most European countries can use their standard licence; others should check whether they need an international licence. Items of horse-riding clothing and equipment that have been used outside Iceland must be disinfected by a vet before travel and you will need to present official proof of this on arrival. Otherwise, the items will be disinfected for you at a cost on arrival.

GETTING AROUND

CAR

The statutory speed limit in built-up areas is 50kmh, on overland roads with gravel surface it's 8 kmh and 90kmh on asphalt. The loose gravel offers vehicles little grip, and you must be careful when swerving to avoid oncoming traffic on the often narrow roads.

Warning signs with the word *"blindhæð"* indicate blind summits on hills. Animals, such as free-roaming sheep, always have right of way in Iceland. It is compulsory to drive with dipped headlights, even during the day. All persons travelling in the vehicle must wear a seatbelt. The blood-alcohol limit is 0%.

For driving in the Highlands, you'll need an off-road vehicle. Use *road.is* to see which routes are open and all the key rules for driving in Iceland. If you drive on such a trail before it has been officially declared open, you can be fined; the police regularly monitor traffic, including from the air. It is also strictly prohibited to drive outside the marked trails.

Apart from in the Highlands, there is a fairly dense network of petrol stations. In Reykjavík and the larger towns, they are generally open until midnight. Here, you can often fill up and pay by card at self-service machines. Unleaded petrol (95 octane and 98 octane) as well as diesel *(dísel)* are available.

CAR HIRE

Almost all larger towns have a car-hire firm. It always pays to compare prices offered by the various companies; the smallest models cost around 9,700 ISK per day in the summer.

Hire cars are relatively new and suited to Icelandic driving conditions. Drivers must be at least 20 years of age – and 23 for off-road vehicles – and have had a driving licence for at least a year. If you take your hire car into the Highlands or on rough, off-road trails, you will be fined accordingly.

PUBLIC TRANSPORT

Iceland has an extensive public bus network, and in the summer months several bus passes are on offer with reduced fares. You can get on and off at any point along the route. Information on tours, timetables, fares and special offers: *Destination Iceland (BSÍ bus station | bsi.is)*.

Strætó is the Reykjavík bus company, with routes outside as well as inside the capital. If you are hoping to travel mostly by bus, it is worth downloading the Strætó app. Information: *straeto.is*.

Download the map at *public transport.is* for a solid overview of bus connections and companies.

Air Iceland and Eagle Air fly to various destinations within Iceland and also offer charter flights. Information: *ernir.is* and *airiceland.is*

FESTIVALS & EVENTS

ALL YEAR ROUND

FEBRUARY

Winter Lights Festival (Reykjavík): light installations across the city; swimming pools stay open late for Pool Night. *winterlightsfestival.is*

MARCH

DesignMarch (Reykjavík): All about design. *designmarch.is*

APRIL

International Literary Festival (Reykjavík): every other year; the next is in 2025. *bokmenntahatid.is*

MAY/JUNE

Reykjavík Arts Festival (Reykjavík): showcasing international and national artists from all genres. Every second year. *listahatid.is*

JUNE

Sailors' Day (nationwide): first weekend in June

Viking Festival (Hafnarfjörður)

JULY

End of the volcanic eruption (Heimaey): first weekend in July

Reykjavík Fringe Festival (Reykjavík): fresh, innovative art from Iceland. *rvkfringe.is*

AUGUST

Gay Pride (Reykjavík)

Reykjavík marathon (Reykjavík): *marathon.is*

Culture Night (Reykajvík): all events are free of charge (photo).

SEPTEMBER

Sheep and horse round-up (across Iceland)

SEPTEMBER/OCTOBER

Reykjavík International Film Festival (Reykjavík): *riff.is*

OCTOBER/NOVEMBER

Iceland Airwaves Festival (Reykjavík): *icelandairwaves.is*

Strætó buses are powered by hydrogen

EMERGENCIES

EMBASSIES

UK EMBASSY

Laufásvegur 31, 101 Reykjavík | tel. 5 505100 | info@britishembassy.is | ukiniceland.fco.gov.uk

US EMBASSY

Laufásvegur 21, 101 Reykjavík | tel. 5 952200 | iceland.usembassy.gov

HEALTH

In the event of serious illness or an accident, you should contact the A&E department *(slysadeild)* at a hospital *(sjúkrahús)* or contact a doctor *(læknir)* directly. Medical bills must be paid in cash. Find out from your medical insurance company before your travel which costs will be covered, and take out separate travel health insurance for your trip, if necessary.

Pharmacies *(apótek)* are recognisable by the sign with a cross and the words *"Lyf og heilsa"*. They are open during normal business hours, and there is usually one on duty around the clock in Reykjavík. If you are dependent on regular medication, be sure to take a sufficient stock with you in case it is not possible to obtain precisely the same products in Iceland.

EMERGENCY CALLS

Nationwide emergency telephone number: 112

ESSENTIALS

ACCOMMODATION

Icelandic accommodation has it all: from options with a thousand stars – that would be a tent – to hostels, guest rooms and luxury hotels. Still, prices are (very) steep in the high season, especially in the capital. All the usual booking platforms are available to book accommodation.

INSIDER TIP **Book direct**

If you want to stay in a four-star hotel, especially in the low season, you will usually find a better deal by booking directly. Four stars for the price of two! With the exception of Radisson SAS and Hilton you will only find Icelandic hotel chains. There are, for example, Icelandair hotels *(icelandairhotels.com)*, which also include the three simple Edda hotels, or Foss hotels *(fosshotel.is)*. Many of them are located in beautiful spots.

Under the name *Hey Iceland (heyiceland.is)*, a number of farms and guesthouses have clubbed together to offer a whole range of activities, from horse-riding and fishing to hunting, swimming and sheep herding, as well as accommodation. Some of these farms also offer the option to rent a holiday home. You can book via Hey Iceland.

A number of tour operators also rent out private summer cottages or holiday apartments, but these often have to be booked for a minimum of one week. Examples include Katla *(katla-travel.is)* and Viator *(viator.is)*.

The number of youth hostels is on the rise. The association's 24 hostels are open to all, with no age restrictions in place. For information and brochures, try the youth hostel association *Bandalag Íslenskra Farfugla (Reykjavík | Sundlaugavegur 34 | tel. 575 6700 | hostel.is)*. There are also plenty of private hostels offering simple accommodation, ofen at lower prices.

There are cabins for hikers to rent from Icelandic hiking clubs *(see Mountaineering, p. 34)*. Best to book in advance.

Iceland has more than 170 campsites. Most are only open from June to August, and standards and facilities vary greatly. On average, you can expect to pay around 2,000 ISK per person per night plus the tent. The annual *Camping Card* gives you access to around 30 sites. Costing 179 euros, it is valid from the opening of the camping season until 15 September and covers two adults and up to four children under 16. You also get a discount at Olís and ÓB petrol stations. *Info: campingcard.is*.

There are many other campsites in smaller places that are not covered by the card. Many are located directly next to a swimming pool *(nat.is/camping-in-iceland)*. Wild camping in a tent or camper van is not permitted.

CLIMATE & WHEN TO TRAVEL

The most popular and busiest time to travel to Iceland is from June to August, when the average daytime temperatures hit 15°C, the likelihood of rain is at its lowest and the days are longest. An ideal holiday time is September, the only true autumnal month, when Iceland is cloaked in myriad golden hues. Another good time to go is May, when the days are long and the first buds and blossoms are appearing. That's also the month of the *Reykjavík Art Festival*, and outdoor life gets under way in earnest. In the winter, it can get very cold on account of the wind; on the other hand, this is the best time for a sighting of the Northern Lights. Iceland is notorious for its changeable weather, so don't forget to pack your waterproofs, sunglasses and a warm jumper.

CUSTOMS

Adults may bring alcohol and cigarettes into the country in appropriate quantities. It is prohibited to bring in animals, narcotics, fresh meat, fresh dairy products and eggs. You'll find detailed information under *tollur.is* You are not permitted to take the following out of Iceland: protected plants, egg shells, birds' eggs or nests, birds, pieces of stone broken out of caves or any other protected natural

RESPONSIBLE TRAVEL

It doesn't take a lot to be environmentally friendly when travelling. Don't just think about your carbon footprint while flying to and from your holiday destination, but also about how you can protect nature and culture abroad. As a tourist it is especially important to respect nature, look out for local products, cycle instead of driving, save water and much more. If you would like to find out more about eco-tourism please visit: *ecotourism.org*

places. Historical or archaeological artefacts may also not be exported.

INFORMATION

Comprehensive information on Iceland, with brochures for downloading: *Icelandic Tourist Office | visit iceland.com*

Ferðamálaráð Íslands | Geirsgata 9, 101 Reykjavík | tel. 535 5500 | visit iceland.com

Icelandic Tourist Board in the USA | c/o Scandinavian Tourist Board, 655 Third Avenue, New York, NY 10017 | tel. 212 8 85 97 00 | visiticeland.com

iceland.is: Iceland's official site showcases nature, culture and the economy. The comprehensive list of links is an excellent source of information.

MONEY

Credit cards are widely accepted. Mastercard and Visa are accepted nationwide. If private individuals will only accept cash, there are plenty of ATMs available. The Icelandic currency is the *króna* (ISK). *See cb.is* for the latest exchange rate. The rate fluctuates regularly.

NATIONAL HOLIDAYS

1 Jan	New Year
March / April	Maundy Thursday, Good Friday Easter Monday
3rd Thu in April	first day of summer
1 May	Labour Day
May/June	Ascension, Whit Monday
17 June	Independence Day
1st Mon in Aug	Bank Holiday
24–26 Dec	Christmas
31 Dec	New Year's Eve

OPENING HOURS

Shops are open as follows: Mon–Fri 9am–6pm, Sat 9am–4pm. Some supermarkets are open 24 hours, 7 days a week. The *Kringlan* shopping centre in Reykjavík and *Smáralind* in Kópavogur have extended opening on Thursdays and are open on Sundays (except in summer). Kiosks *(sjópa)* are usually open for business until 11.30pm, selling drinks and a small range of foods.

PHONES & MOBILES

With the exception of companies and the authorities, no one in Iceland uses a landline these days. Almost all visitors now have roaming; research this in advance and have it set up if necessary. You can buy prepaid cards with a corresponding SIM and Icelandic number from the telephone company *Síminn (tel. 800 7000 for information)*. These are also available at petrol stations and kiosks. The mobile network now covers the whole of Iceland with the exception of some very remote Highland regions; coverage at *Síminn (siminn.is)*.

Telephone calls to Iceland: dial 00354, then the seven-digit number. Calling from Iceland: UK 0044, USA 001, then the area code without the 0.

PRICES & TIPPING

Prices are a good deal higher than the rest of Europe. Alcoholic beverages are particularly expensive. *Bónus* shops are the cheapest place to buy groceries if you plan on self catering.

Tips are included in the price at restaurants, and Icelanders don't add extra. Many tourists still give an additional tip, but it is not expected.

HOW MUCH DOES IT COST?

Bus ride	*£3.10 for a ticket on Reykjavík's buses*
Souvenir	*from £133 for an Icelandic pullover*
Beer	*from £5.30 for a half-litre in a bar*
Coffee	*from £2 for two cups*
Snack	*£1.75 for a skyr with fruit*
Swimming pool	*£7 admission charge in Reykjavík*

WEATHER IN REYKJAVÍK

High season
Low season

	JAN	FEB	MARCH	APRIL	MAY	JUNE	JULY	AUG	SEPT	OCT	NOV	DEC
Daytime temperature	2°	3°	5°	6°	10°	13°	15°	14°	12°	8°	5°	4°
Night-time temperature	-3°	-3°	-1°	1°	4°	7°	9°	8°	6°	3°	0°	-2°
Sunshine hours/day	1	2	4	5	7	5	7	6	4	3	2	1
Rainy days/month	14	12	12	12	10	10	10	12	13	14	14	15
Water temperature in °C	4°	4°	4°	5°	7°	9°	11°	11°	10°	7°	6°	5°

Sunshine hours/day Rainy days/month Water temperature in °C

WORDS & PHRASES IN ICELANDIC

MISCELLANEOUS

yes/no	já/nei
please/thank you	gerðu svo vel/takk fyrir
Excuse me!	Afsakið!
Hello!/Good evening!	Góðan daginn!/Gott kvöld!
Goodbye!	Vertu sæll! (to men)/Vertu sæl! (to women)
Bye! (informal)	Bless!
I am called ...	Eg heiti ...
I come from ...	Eg er frá ...
... the UK	... Stóra-Bretland
... the USA	... Bandaríkin
I can't understand you	Eg skil ekki neitt
How much does it cost?	Hvað kostar það?
Excuse me, where is ...?	Afsakið, hvar er ...?
1/2/3/4/5/6/7/8/9/10/20/100	einn/tveir/þrír/fjórir/fimm/sex/sjö/átta/níu/tíu/tuttugu/hundrað

SYMBOLS

Signpost in the hiking area between Þórsmörk and Eyjafjallajökull

FOR BOOKWORMS & FILM BUFFS

BETRAYAL
Lilja Sigurðiardóttir's crime novels expose dark machinations at play in Iceland. In this latest thriller, an interior minister is burnt to death (2022).

ICELAND'S BELL
Nobel laureate Halldór Laxness's novel is both a modern take on the traditional Icelandic saga and an ascerbic social satire (1943).

LAMB
Debut film from Icelandic director Valdimir Jóhannsson, with Noomi Rapace and Hilmir Snær Guðnason. A mystical and melancholy telling of a story of a special lamb (2022).

KALMANN
Jochen Schmidt's hero is one of a kind. Set in Raufarhöfn, the novel is full of surprises and secrets (2020).

TRAPPED
Five-part TV series from Baltasar Kormákur. Trouble comes to wintry Siglúfjördur, cut off from the rest of the world. Absolutely dark and truly thrilling (2017).

PLAYLIST ON SHUFFLE

0:58

SAMARIS – R4VIN
Björk is obsessed with the band – admittedly their sound is not all that dissimilar from her early work.

ASDFHG – STEYPA
Steinunn Jónsdóttir sings in shimmering style to her electronic music. A great talent discovered at the Sónar music festival in 2016.

SIGUR RÓS – STARÁLFUR
Song from their second album, *Ágætis Byrjun*, which skyrocketed the group to worldwide fame.

JÓN LEIFS – GEYSIR
Every stage in a geyser's activity realised by an orchestra.

SIGRÚN – VÍTAHRINGUR
Sigrún creates experimental industrial music with abstract harmonies. Fun for some!

Your holiday soundtrack can be found on **Spotify** under **MARCO POLO Iceland**

Or scan this code with the Spotify app

ONLINE

ICELANDIC COUPONS
This app offers coupons and money-saving tips – excellent for the thrifty! After all, Iceland is not exactly cheap...

VEDUR
Iceland's go-to weather app, run by the Meteorological Office and including hazard warnings. The weather can change very quickly here.

APPY HOUR
This app from free magazine *Grapevine* makes for a fun evening out in Reykjavík.

I HEART REYKJAVÍK
A travel blog all about Iceland, seen through the eyes of a local. You can book tours and more on the site. *iheartreykjavik.net*

GPSMYCITY APP REYKJAVÍK
The app shows a number of Reykjavík sites, as well as maps for themed city tours, like Museums, Shopping or Nightlife.

TRAVEL PURSUIT

THE MARCO POLO HOLIDAY QUIZ

Do you know what makes Iceland tick? Here you can test your knowledge of the little secrets and idiosyncrasies of the country and its people. You will find the correct answers below, with further details on pages 15 to 23 of this guide.

❶ Which European "discovered" America?

a) Erik the Red
b) Leifur Eiríksson
c) Marco Polo

❷ How is power generated in Iceland?

a) Wind, since it's so stormy
b) Water, as there's so much of it
c) Water and geothermal, because two is better than one!

❸ How many sheep are there in the country?

a) Twice as many as people: approx. 700,000
b) One sheep for every Icelander: approx. 350,000
c) Icelanders are happy to share: approx. 400,000

❹ What are Einar Jóhannsson's children called?

a) Jórunn and Gísli Jóhannsson
b) Jórunn Einarsdóttir and Gísli Einarsson
c) Jórunn Johannsdóttir and Gísli Jóhannsson

Answers: 1b, 2c, 3c, 4b, 5a, 6b, 7b, 8c, 9a, 10c, 11a

How many sheep live in Iceland?

❺ Which land mammals were brought to Iceland by settlers?

a) All of them, except for foxes
b) Just rats and mice, those classic ship stowaways
c) Just cows and sheep

❻ How do Icelanders heat their homes?

a) With oil and gas, hence the large tanks everywhere
b) With hot water and electricity
c) With electricity

❼ What does *"Þetta reddast"* mean?

a) What will be will be
b) We'll manage
c) That's a problem

❽ Where do the elves live?

a) In trees, which is why their numbers are growing
b) In volcanoes
c) In rocks and boulders

❾ What did former mayor of Reykjavík Jón Gnarr oriignally do for a living?

a) Author and comedian
b) Owner of a private bank
c) Lawyer

❿ How old is Iceland in geological terms?

a) Around 100 million years old
b) 200–250 million years old
c) 15–20 million years old

⓫ What is lava used for?

a) Building, especially roads
b) Baking
c) Countryside tennis courts

INDEX

WE WANT TO HEAR FROM YOU!

Did you have a great holiday? Is there something on your mind? Whatever it is, let us know! Whether you want to praise the guide, alert us to errors or give us a personal tip – MARCO POLO would be pleased to hear from you.

Please contact us by email:

sales@heartwoodpublishing.co.uk

We do everything we can to provide the very latest information for your trip. Nevertheless, despite all of our authors' thorough research, errors can creep in. MARCO POLO does not accept any liability for this.

PICTURE CREDITS

Cover photo: At the entrance to a glacier cave (huber-images: T. Mackie)

Photos: Author S. Barth (139); huber-images: M. Delpho (32/33), S. Kremer (27, 54/55), M. Rellini (front outside flap, front inside flap, 1, 95, 107), M. Robertz (66), B. Römmelt (10); laif: M. Amme (20), M. Galli (38/39), G. Haenel (9), M. Kirchgessner (78/79), T. Linkel (30/31, 86, 119); laif/hemis.fr: Boisberranger (31), Rieger (8); laif/Le Figaro Magazine: Gladieu (11); laif/robertharding: P. Dieudonne (90/91); Look/age fotostock (89); Look/SagaPhoto (2/3, 136/137); mauritius images: C. Lutz (45), C. Lux (77), M. Runkel (96), I. van der Weil (63); mauritius images/age: L. Castañeda (14/15), R. T. Sigurdsson (60, 82); mauritius images/Alamy: A. Bezuglov (124/125), E. Bjarnason (85), C. Ehlers (49), F. Fuxa (109), J. Lombardo (24/25), R. T. Sigurdsson (43, 100/101, 127); mauritius images/Alamy/Arctic Images (128); mauritius images/Alamy/HomoCosmicos (74); mauritius images/Alamy/maxoliki (59); mauritius images/Alamy/Megapress (134/135); mauritius images/Alamy/RooM the Agency (back flap); mauritius images/Arctic-Images (28, 99, 102/103); mauritius images/Aurora Photos: A. Peacock (12/13); mauritius images/Cultura: Henn Photography (26/27), G. Karbus Photography (19); mauritius images/imageBroker: O. Krüger (112); mauritius images/John Warburton-Lee: W. Gray (35); mauritius images/Novarc Images: N. Alexander Otto (73); mauritius images/Prisma: M. Galli (52); mauritius images/Westend61: M. Benik (114/115); shutterstock: basiczto (46), Rita_R Gentile (6/7), GuilhermeMesquita (110), S. Hawks (68/69), silky (23), O. Troino (64), Lenka Pribanova (133)

3rd Edition – fully revised and updated 2024
Worldwide Distribution: Heartwood Publishing Ltd, Bath, United Kingdom
www.heartwoodpublishing.co.uk

Authors: Sabine Barth
Editor: Martin Silbermann
Picture editor: Susanne Mack
Cartography: © MAIRDUMONT, Ostfildern (pp. 40–41, 116, 120, 122, outside jacket, pull-out map; © MAIRDUMONT, Ostfildern, using data from OpenStreetMap, licence CC-BY-SA 2.0 (pp. 40–41, 51, 56–57, 70–71, 80–81, 92–93, 104–105)
Cover design and pull-out map cover design: bilekjaeger_Kreativagentur with Zukunftswerkstatt, Stuttgart
Page design: Langenstein Communication GmbH, Ludwigsburg

Heartwood Publishing credits:
Translated from the German by Madeleine Taylor Laidler, Jennifer Walcoff Neuheiser, Tübingen, Susan Jones, Tübingen
Editors: Rosamund Sales, Kate Michell
Prepress: Summerlane Books, Bath
Printed in India

MARCO POLO AUTHOR

SABINE BARTH

A trip to Iceland is an annual must for Sabine Barth, not least because there is always something new to discover in this ever-changing country – including its geology! Barth has been travelling to Iceland since 1981 and lived on the island for several years. Smitten by the country and its stunning landscapes on her first visit, she has been writing and talking about Iceland, its people and culture for print media and radio ever since.

DOS & DON'TS

HOW TO AVOID SLIP-UPS & BLUNDERS

DON'T TRAVEL IN HIGH SEASON

Everyone loves the summer, but if you want to experience Iceland at its most natural, it's best not to travel during the high season. At other times, even in winter, Iceland can truly live up to its reputation of offering you nature at its finest.

DO TAKE OFF YOUR SHOES

When you enter an Icelandic home, you should usually take off your shoes. Only leave them on if your host tells you to. It's definitely more polite to take them off!

DON'T SHOWER IN SWIMWEAR

In swimming pools, you are explicitly requested to shower – without your bathing costume – before swimming. Icelandic pools are not treated with chlorine, and for this reason, hygiene is a top priority. So just do as the Icelanders do and you won't automatically stick out as being a tourist.

DO GET DRESSED UP

The Icelanders set great store by looking well-groomed, and dress with the appropriate degree of elegance when they go out. For Reykjavík, especially, it makes good sense to pack a few items of clothing for evenings as well as hiking gear.

DON'T DISTURB THE BIRDS

Photographing and filming the nests of endangered species, such as eagles, falcons, snowy owls and little auks, is punishable by law. A much better idea is to buy yourself one of the excellent illustrated bird books available.